How Dare
You Manage?

How Dare You Manage?

Seven Principles
to Close the CEO Skill Gap

NICK FORREST

BPS books

Toronto & New York
www.bpsbooks.com

Published in 2013 by
BPS Books
Toronto & New York
www.bpsbooks.com
A division of Bastian Publishing Services Ltd.

ISBN 978-1-927483-69-5

Cataloguing-in-Publication Data available from Library
and Archives Canada.

HOW DARE YOU MANAGE is a registered trademark of Nick Forrest.
CORMORANT MANAGEMENT and CEO MANAGEMENT
PRINCIPLES are trademarks of Nick Forrest.

Cover: Michael Clark/Daniel Crack
Text design and typesetting: Daniel Crack, Kinetics Design, kdbooks.ca
Graphic illustrations: Lori Harrison
Index: Gillian Watts

To Sally.
How lucky I am!

CONTENTS

Preface

I have written *How Dare You Manage?* to help would-be, new or veteran CEOs to close what I call the CEO skill gap. This gap exists because those who reach the very top of their organization:

- Have never been taught how to manage large groups of employees
- Have never been accountable for *everything* (until now, they have always worked for someone else – there was always a boss to defer to)
- Believe their role is to lead, whereas – and this may sound counterintuitive – it is primarily to *manage*

While I address CEOs directly throughout this book, I have written it for many others, as well, including:

- Executive vice presidents or vice presidents, some of whom may aspire to the top role, who run a division in excess of 250 employees
- Anyone who is part of an executive team that collectively manages a large workforce
- Board members (including the chair of the nominating committee) who work with executive leaders and CEOs. Members of a company's board are custodians of the company; they should understand what it takes to support those who manage large groups of employees
- Individuals who have been identified by the senior leadership team as high potential. Leaders and board members should be proactive in inviting senior talent in to the boardroom. If you are invited, you need to understand corporate leadership; you need to display how, in your department, you are doing all of the things that would be required of you in the CEO's position: developing and implementing a clear structure

for your department and a functioning succession-planning strategy, setting and defining the goals of your department and reaching them through your people, and, most importantly, aligning your department with company-wide goals and approaches

- Anyone who consults for, or provides services to, members of the C-suite (this includes executive coaches)
- Senior Human Resources managers

Furthermore, while I focus on the realities of corporate life, readers in other types of business will also find this book helpful, including heads of family businesses and entrepreneurs/owners.

How Dare You Manage? includes examples from my experience as a consultant to CEOs and other senior leaders. In particular, I follow the progress of Jos Wintermans of Canadian Tire Acceptance Ltd., who provides a powerful illustration of how CEOs can identify their skill gap and close it – and the amazing results that follow.

Allow me to speak to you, my reader, directly. I believe this book will help you focus on learning the *craft*, as opposed to the *techniques*, of management. (Say goodbye to the management flavour of the month.) I believe you will experience an increase in confidence by knowing there is a proven way forward, and "I can do this." I hope your enthusiasm will spike at the possibility that "I can truly create a highly productive organization that can achieve spectacular results with an engaged, kick-ass workforce."

Above all, I hope my boldness in identifying a skill gap in top leaders as one of the most serious problems faced by organizations today will be taken in the spirit in which it is meant: to help you unlock your own potential and the potential of *everyone* you manage.

Nick Forrest

PART ONE

The Gap

CHAPTER ONE

It's the CEO Skill Gap That Needs Closing

How dare you manage®?

I rarely say this aloud when I'm consulting for CEOs, senior managers and board members, but it is often on the tip of my tongue.

Why? Because the corporate landscape today is replete with top leaders who don't understand it is now their work to manage a large group of people. They don't know what is required for doing so: developing and implementing a clear structure, process and set of practices for managers and those they manage, and executing on these consistently. This management deficit is a serious matter. Senior leaders who lack this understanding, who lack this skill, do untold damage to their organization: they hurt not only their employees but also the prospects of their organization and of themselves, not to mention their customers' trust. Customers have always voted with their feet, but today they don't wait long to verify their perceptions, and they don't walk; they run.

Ironically, chief executive officers often tell their executive leadership team, board members, shareholders and the media that their organization is being held back by a skill gap among their employees. This almost always sounds good and right. And what happens next is logical, as policies and programs are developed to:

- Find, train and retain the best talent and align the talent with the company's products or services
- Teach everyone in the company to work collaboratively with customers
- Ensure that all of the company's internal and external communications underscore this approach

I contend, however, that, to move forward, companies and boards, and CEOs themselves, must address a prior skill gap: the *CEO skill gap.*

Who Trains CEOs to Be CEOs?

It has become painfully clear to me, in my twenty-five years as a consultant to the C-suite, that business does not teach managers how to be a CEO.

Why?

Partly because the aura surrounding the position almost guarantees that CEOs will not hear what they need to hear. Even from themselves.

Partly because some CEOs approach their role politically. They litter the battlefield with anyone who gets in their way, including those whose wisdom they so sorely need. If these CEOs have a gap, they don't notice it – and even if they did, it's doubtful that they would care.

And partly – mainly – because it has never occurred to most CEOs that there is a significant difference between managing a group of employees in part of an organization and managing *all* of the employees in the entire organization.

But there is good news. If I am right that a misconception about their role is behind the CEO skill gap, then CEOs who have the courage and tenacity to address and redress that misconception will release enormous amounts of talent and energy in the organization they lead.

▼▼▼

In the next two chapters, I deal with three key insights that *you* as a CEO or aspiring CEO need to have about your own skill gap (chapter 2) and the necessity for you to see management as a lifelong craft, not a series of ever-changing, and often arbitrary, techniques (chapter 3). These chapters will prepare you for the second and third parts of the book, in which I discuss seven essential CEO management principles™ (note: I call these *CEO* management principles, to distinguish them from general management practices) and show you how to apply them so you can guide, focus, control and manage the direction of large numbers of employees and achieve great results – and get lots of feedback from those employees while you're at it.

By doing this, you will:

- Become a successful CEO
- Win a reputation as a manager capable of positively transforming organizations and lives
- Build a sustainable organization – one that transcends you
- Set your company on a path of innovation and creative problem solving
- Watch your organization become sustainably profitable

Executive Summary

1. CEOs are in danger of never hearing what they need to hear.

2. Most CEOs were never trained to be a CEO.

3. Most CEOs do not understand that they now lead a very large group of people: *all of the employees* in their organization.

4. Addressing and redressing this misconception will help CEOs release the talents and energy of their entire workforce.

CHAPTER TWO

Three Key Insights into the CEO Skill Gap

Closing a gap requires knowing what it is. This chapter offers three insights that I believe will help you recognize and understand your skill gap. The insights you need to have are:

- Now I have *more*, not fewer, people to manage
- Now I'm accountable for everything – yes, *everything*
- Now I need to *manage* more, as opposed to leading more

Key Insight #1:
Now I Have *More*, not Fewer, People to Manage

In your development years as a young manager, and as you rose through the ranks of the companies where you worked, you learned to manage ever-larger groups of direct reports – teams of 20, 50, 60, 70 or even 150. But nobody sat you down and taught you how to manage 250, 750, 1,500, 3,000, 5,000, 25,000 or more employees. Eventually the day came when you got the nod and were promoted to run a division or even a whole company with a large workforce.

In my experience, the more honest of the leaders in this situation admit after a month or so that they:

- Didn't (and, in many cases, still don't) have a clue how to manage such a large group
- Don't understand the frame of reference and how to integrate the structure, processes, policies, skills and knowledge they need to confidently lead and manage their organization
- Don't know, now that they're working on this larger canvas, how to attain a level of competitive capability that will enable the consistent achievement of great results with a more capable and more engaged workforce

The reason for this is simple. Most who gain admission to the C-suite believe they now have *fewer* employees to manage and interact with, and a select few, at that: the members of their senior leadership team and the board of directors. "Manage the company? I have people for that." This is pretty close to how some CEOs see it. It's all too easy for them to believe that they have just been rewarded for *their* managerial work by being given a position that transcends management. Is this how you feel?

When I ask CEOs and managers how many employees they have, most of them respond with the number of their direct reports (six, eight or ten) and not the total number (250, 500, 1,000, 4,000, 25,000 or more). Actually, most CEOs don't even know the total number of their employees.

Never forget that when you take on the leadership of a large number of employees, you are accountable for the environment in which they work. You will never stop thinking about your employees and how to raise their collective level of capability and enthusiasm to implement your strategy. As CEO, you are accountable to leave your company stronger than when you found it.

Enter CEO Jos Wintermans

One CEO, Jos Wintermans, was fortunate to see through this misconception. First, he realized that his primary responsibility was to all of the company's employees, not just his leadership team and board. And second, he understood that "managing 700 employees is an entirely different ballgame from managing 100." This thought had niggled at the back of his mind in the few months since he had taken over as president of Canadian Tire Acceptance Ltd. (CTAL), the independent credit card arm of the national retailer. Now, as the windows of his corner office darkened in the dimming Niagara winter evening, the thought rushed to the forefront of his mind.

It was January 1988. Wintermans was the first CEO of CTAL to follow the founder, who had led it for twenty-five years. Although CTAL had been an early innovator, it had stagnated over the years.

The board, dissatisfied with performance in recent years, was pressing Wintermans to significantly increase both sales and profits. Wintermans had taken on the role gladly, his first in the top position. He had spent his first two months meeting employees, walking the floors, reviewing the existing situation and working with the executive group to assess the status quo and the way ahead. Now he wondered if he would be able to turn the company around before the board decided to find someone else to lead.

CTAL required a major transformation to fulfill the board's expectations. Problems were everywhere. The company strategy, best described as "more of the same," was not likely to yield the expected results. The calcified executive team couldn't or wouldn't work together. Decision-making was painfully slow. Major projects came in late and over budget. Employees were disengaged. Effort and effectiveness went unrewarded; sometimes it was even punished. And it seemed that, as far as the managers were concerned, the people you curled or golfed with mattered more than your performance.

Thinking about the change and challenge ahead, Wintermans realized how little expertise he had to run such a large number of employees. The scale of things was just so different from what it had been in his previous management roles.

It wasn't that he lacked experience. Wintermans had been a high-achieving manager. Strengthened with advanced degrees in both law and business, he had taken the traditional mobile career of an up-and-coming executive. His success as a junior executive at American Express Canada attracted the attention of the Canadian Tire board. He knew the ins and outs of the credit card industry, the requirements of retail outlets and the needs of consumers. He had a solid mastery of everything taught in MBA courses about management and the technical aspects of the chief executive's job: financial reporting, accounting, budgeting, employment law, taxation and so on. But this mastery, sufficient for success in lower ranks, was proving to be woefully unhelpful at the top.

"I had an impression of disquiet the first time I walked through the Welland, Ontario, headquarters and saw everyone sitting there," he recalls. "I had a flashback to when I was twelve years old and was visiting my uncle's small cigar manufacturing plant in a village in Belgium. I remembered a sense of profound silence in a large room of three hundred people. They didn't talk, didn't appear to be engaged in any way, looked very serious and sat quietly working, cutting and rolling cigars.

"When I did my introductory walk-around at CTAL, I thought, 'I have seen this picture before, and I don't like this' – but I was at a loss as to what to do. I knew if I messed up, all of these people would be out of a job, a situation that would reverberate throughout the entire community. So my task was to ensure that we did well and give employees an opportunity to do good work. As we said later, we want people driving into our parking lot looking forward to the day's work at CTAL."

So Wintermans sat in his office that January evening and wondered what he had taken on.

"In every tough assignment," Wintermans told me later, "there can be a moment when you reach a nadir of despair and lack of self-confidence about what you face. I realized I didn't know what to do. I didn't have the experience, skills or knowledge to manage through this challenge. I had no experience about how to manage large groups of employees. What I had was plenty of experience managing small groups: I could get my hands around 100 employees, but 700-plus employees was a completely different ballgame. I asked myself, 'How do I align, integrate, engage and motivate 700 employees to deliver the strategy I have in mind?'"

A Common Experience Once at the Top

Wintermans' story likely will resonate with you; certainly it is similar to the experience of so many executives I have encountered. When I talk to my clients about how they grew in their experience and capability, they usually say it developed along these lines: "I got promoted to manager, and then I had to figure it out on my own."

Their careers were a series of assignments of managing increasing numbers of employees. The work was transactional and operational. Like Wintermans, these executives learned the basics of general management. They went to competency training and were given bigger and bigger assignments. They grew in their technical competence, but not in the skills of managing very large groups. They were told that leadership mattered, but nobody defined the difference between leadership and management. They worked hard and got things done, moving progressively up the career ladder to executive.

Eventually, they got the tap on the shoulder for the big one. The more honest of our clients admit this was a "now what?" moment. They were expected to hit the ground running, but, like Wintermans, they began to see that achieving success in managing a large organization of 250 or more was very different from how they had achieved success in their earlier roles.

The Captain Who Thought He Had Control

When it comes to managing their employees, most CEOs operate much like the ship captain in a story I heard years ago from the writer Peter Block.

The captain stands at the helm of a massive ship. Changing the direction of something so large takes a great deal of time and effort, with a big lag between command and result. The captain barks orders into a microphone to the crew below.

Unfortunately, the intercom system is busted. The two sailors in charge of moving the rudder have discovered where the beer is kept and are having a good time drinking it. Every now and then they move the rudder. Every once in a while this coincides with the direction the captain, disconnected on the bridge, has ordered. Seeing the ship finally go in his direction, the captain glows with pride and thinks, *I command this ship!*

Figure 1

Likewise, most CEOs think they have control, but do they? Their organizational ship occasionally heads in the direction they want, and they think they made this happen. In reality, in most cases the levers in their hands aren't connected to anything. Or if they are, they are capable of causing only the crudest of adjustments. These CEOs pound away at these clumsy controls even when they can do nothing to alter the course of their company. If communication works at all, it works poorly. Little goes down, and little comes back up.

Figure 2: How many employees do you have?

Ask yourself why you have the number of employees you have in the first place. (It always surprises me when a CEO I'm working with does not know how many people work in the organization they manage.) Presumably you value your employees as an essential asset to enable you to implement your strategy. Very few employees come to work intending to mess up or do sub-standard work. But it's amazing how many obstacles an organization can put in their way, obstacles that seem explicitly designed to make them less than fully effective. When this happens, it's bad for your organization (paying for sub-optimal work) and bad for your employees (working in an environment that is dispiriting and leads to long-term loss of motivation, pride, self-confidence and self-worth).

For corporations, after all, are social entities. Originally, they were granted the rights they have – such as limited liability – in return for the social and economic benefits they brought. Unless these social obligations are respected, society will revoke these rights. Look at all of the angst in connection with the fall of Nortel. In this case, many inside and outside the company felt that senior management betrayed their social contract. That the people at the top levels looked after their own financial well-being but hung out thousands of employees to dry, losing them the business and, with it, their pension funds.

You will not necessarily be your management team's best friend. Your goal should be to pursue a long-term view of building the best possible organization, one in which you can manage your employees, enabling them to flourish in their work and deliver great results. They deserve to work in the most effective and efficient organization you can create, managed by the most capable management team you can build. Most employees will spend more time at work than they do with their family. It's immoral for you to allow your organization to become an unfair, inefficient place to work. It should not become a detention camp. (More on this later.)

I'll never forget standing with a CEO in his eighth-floor boardroom as he pointed out the window to show me his number-one problem. We watched as his employees rounded the corner of a large building at a good clip and then caught sight of their own building. To a person, they slowed their gait, lowered their gaze and trudged the rest of the way to the entrance.

"What do I do to fix *that*?" he asked me.

Do you want to be a CEO responsible for a workplace that is degrading to the human spirit?

Key Insight #2:
Now I'm Accountable for Everything –
Yes, *Everything*

Until now, you have always worked for someone else. You have implemented someone else's strategy. You may have influenced the strategy, but you were not accountable for its overall creation, implementation and success. Until now, you have worked within a structure and a set of policies that were determined and approved by someone else.

When you became a CEO, however, you transitioned to a position in which you are accountable for everything.

New CEOs usually understand that they are accountable for the creation and execution of their organization's strategy. But they miss the fact that they are accountable for actually creating or recreating the *structure* of their organization. (It's true that the first act of many CEOs is to restructure, but usually their efforts are relegated to their senior leadership team.) Organizational structure is the key to unlocking the potential performance of hundreds or thousands of employees. It is up to the CEO to define and build it. The top leader's lack of experience and knowledge may cripple an organization's future performance. It's easier to say this than to do it, but I'll say it anyway: *CEOs have to think like CEOs.*

Those who reach the top of their company often continue to think like the managers-of-the-part they were before they got there. They think they still have a management role *within* their company, that they just have a different slice of the pie to manage: their organization's senior leadership team and board of directors.

You must understand that you have not gone from managing one slice of the pie to managing a different slice. Now you manage *the whole pie*. Yes, you are to be a blue-sky policy leader. Yes, your role is to project an image of the company – to give confidence to shareholders and potential investors. Yes, your leadership team demands a great deal of your attention. But your main role is to be a manager-of-the-whole. Of *everything*.

Key Insight #3:
Now I Need to *Manage* More, Not Lead More

The higher you rise in an organization, and the more employees you influence, the more management matters. Management – what I will call CEO management – enables you to achieve the work of your organization. (See figure 3.)

Unfortunately, *leadership* continues to be the hot topic in management writing. "We need leaders, not managers!" is the cri de coeur. Leadership seems sexier and more seductive than management. It is a siren call. But management is more important: it makes results happen through large groups of employees. You can spend time exhorting and encouraging employees as a leader, but unless you manage the entire organization and continuously improve their immediate environment to enable them to get their work done efficiently and effectively, you won't get the high levels of productivity from the huge investment you have made in them.

I'm not saying that leadership is unimportant. I'm saying that management is *more* important.

Leadership and management are probably the most ambiguous words in the world of business; everybody has their own definitions. Your definition may differ from mine. Here's how I define them:

Leadership is face-to-face work, creating a company's vision for the way ahead. Leadership segues from this task to engaging employees in conversations that enlist them in implementing this strategy. Leaders point the way.

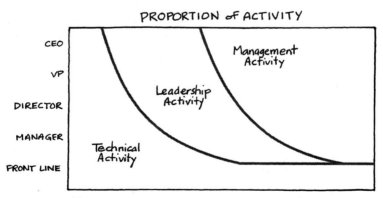

Management matters more than leadership the higher you get in the organization

Figure 3: When management matters more.

CEO management really matters when you can no longer do it face-to-face. It is the design and management of your employees' environment to maximize their understanding of their work, to maximize their efficiency, effectiveness and capability to get work done. Management makes things happen. The larger the group of employees, the more important management is.

Here's an example.

You are the CEO of a 700-employee company. You have 600 front-line employees servicing clients in various roles. One team plans the optimization of truckloads for customer order delivery. There are eight employees reporting to one manager. Young, eager, wanting to make a difference, they were excited when you appointed a new VP of Logistics, who engaged them in division-wide town hall meetings to talk about their future vision and how the division was going to excel in the future. They were told they would have to do more with less, but new systems and processes would enable them to cope.

That was eighteen months ago. Since then, the eight members of the team have attended two more town hall meetings to listen to their VP tell the same story. But nothing has changed for them. In fact, things have grown worse. The employees have lost respect for their manager, they are unclear about expectations for their work and they feel the resources they have are inadequate for successfully completing their work. They have all become frustrated and disengaged. Two have walked out, having come to the realization that they are smarter than their manager. Three others are *this close* to resigning.

And this microcosm of eight employees actually reflects how the majority of their 600 peers feel.

The solution to these challenges is found in management. As CEO, you are accountable to create an environment in which all employees can do their best work. You do this by managing them through a set of management systems designed to help them be efficient, effective and engaged.

All employees should have a manager who can add value to their work. This requires you, as CEO, to manage a fit-to-role / succession-planning process that consistently reviews and assesses your managers to a T. The result? Your company will have a highly capable team of managers who can build a highly engaged workforce. But here's the point: you achieve this through management, not leadership.

The key leverage to your effectiveness is to identify the obstacles that hinder your employees' effectiveness and then implement the required management systems to overcome them. In the long term, employees do not really care how charismatic you are as a leader. They care about their immediate environment and their ability to do their work. Fix these immediate challenges for them, and you will have highly engaged employees. I repeat: to do this, *management* matters more than *leadership*.

If he had relied simply on charismatic leadership, Jos Wintermans could not have solved his problem. He needed something more than inspiring his people to new heights. He needed to learn how to manage a large organization and unlock the imprisoned potential of his employees.

Figure 4 charts the evolution of a CEO from manager of ever-increasing numbers of reports and complexity of activity. It is very important for you to note that a fully evolved manager ... is still a manager.

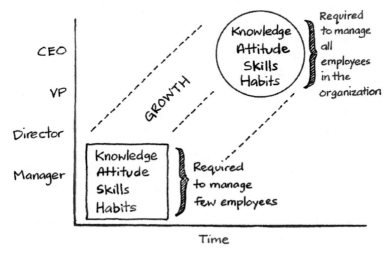

Figure 4: The evolution of a CEO's ability to manage beyond face-to-face engagement.

This figure shows how knowledge, attitude, skills and habits (KASH)* will enable managers of a division to achieve what they do today. But a radically different inventory of KASH is required for them to go from managing a team of 5 to 20 employees to managing 25,000+ employees.

Managers with small groups of employees focus on hands-on directives, immediate problem solving and the achievement of tangible results through short-term transactional work. They can recover quickly when the hinges fall off. Working all hours will solve issues and deliver results. Delivering these tangibles leads to promotion and larger commands.

When they become a director, they manage 50 or more employees or a considerably more diverse portfolio of tasks. Completion times are longer and the criteria for success are more abstract. Effective communication and delegation become more important. Aligning and integrating the work of the department becomes critical. Directors depend on other departments to help them get this work done and meet their goals. But they still can avert or control a crisis through hands-on efforts.

But when they're promoted to managing 250+, they enter a whole new world of complexity. Now they are accountable to harness and marshal large groups of employees to achieve a complex, long-term strategy, and all this in the face of a host of socio-economic and competitive threats.

This new world requires them to value, understand and manage the implementation of a corporate methodology: a set of integrated practices and policies that empower, engage and energize employees so they can truly contribute to achieving the corporate strategy. In other words, the number of employees they now manage has the bulge on them. No longer can they manage the way they used to. Their discipline, knowledge, skills, confidence and habits have to grow and change.

Where are you in this process? The higher you are, the more your challenges and goals go from short-term tactical and concrete to long-term strategic and abstract. To meet them will require you to

---

* A concept developed by The Strategic Coach®.

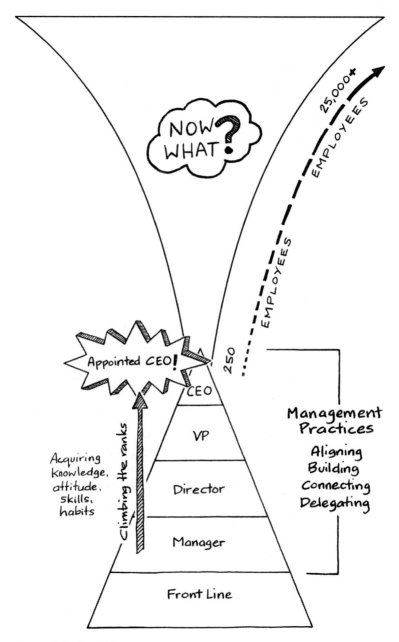

Figure 5: Half a CEO.

think differently. You are organizing and ordering work that will be achieved by others, not by you, over long periods of time. You have moved from operational challenges with concrete objectives to strategic challenges that are abstract, intangible, opaque, murky and interconnected in obscure ways. You must bring order to potential chaos by aligning, integrating and directing the work of the organization. These behaviours become the key requirement of your role to ensure the success of your company. It's your new level of KASH.

Your Problem? You Are Half a CEO

The above three insights should lead you to conclude that you need a set of management principles. You have the first half of what you need as a CEO: the practices you learned as a manager working your way up the organization to become a CEO. Now you need the other half: a complete set of *CEO* management principles. You need more KASH, the knowledge, attitudes, skills and habits required to manage as a CEO.

The problem for Jos Wintermans when he started in the top position was that he was only half a CEO. He understood what it took to manage up to 250 employees. He had mastered management practices for smaller groups of direct reports. He had no reason to believe that anything else was required, but he was aware that he had to deliver results like never before.

Was he so different from you in your first executive assignment? Most CEOs report being surprised by how different the requirements of the role are from what helped them succeed earlier. That's what Leslie Braksick and James Hillgren found when they interviewed twenty-seven top CEOs for the Heinz Company's book *Preparing CEOs for Success*.

Said one CEO, "Core accountabilities like capital allocation, resource deployment, strategy formulation, and leadership development are all learnable parts of the job. Those are the things I have learned to do over time. What are the most challenging are the soft things – these are harder to learn."[1]

Your job of creating and implementing the strategy of your company will not be successful unless your employees do the right work as effectively and efficiently as possible.

General management practices got you to the CEO's office, but they are insufficient to help you solve the challenges you will encounter in the top job. You need the other half of management required for working effectively as an executive: a set of *CEO management principles*.

These principles are discussed in detail in the second part of this book. But before we get to them, there's something very important for you to understand first: that being an effective CEO involves mastering the *craft* of management, as opposed to mastering various free-floating techniques of management. Or let me put it this way:

- The higher you go in an organization, the more management matters over leadership
- Management is a craft, and CEOs are custodians of this craft
- To be a great CEO requires lifelong learning
- It takes courage to seize the day and become a great CEO

So let us turn now to the craft of CEO management.

Executive Summary

1. Always think about the total number of employees in your organization.

2. Now you have more, not fewer, people to manage.

3. Now you're accountable for everything – yes, everything!

4. Now you need to *manage* more, not lead more.

5. You need a different set of management skills as you rise through the organization. What got you to the CEO role will not keep you there.

6. Your ultimate challenge is complexity. Complexity is your friend if you can master it better than your competitors do. To solve complex issues you need to enlist your entire organization. It is no longer just about you.

CHAPTER THREE

The Craft of CEO Management

Did you know that the root of the word "management" is *manus*, which is Latin for "hand"? The hand of the manager certainly is ubiquitous in our time. Take a look around where you're reading this book. From the airplane you took, to the building you're in to the coffee you're drinking and the cleanliness of the area where you're sitting, not to mention the chair you're sitting on and the clothes you're wearing – nothing is planned, created or delivered without the influence, to some degree, of management.

Management is the most important function to have emerged through society's industrialization and evolution to the complex cultures and economies of today. You could be forgiven for doubting this, for today managers are viewed, often for good reason, as the tools of capitalist exploiters and are ridiculed by union leaders as insensitive abusers of unprotected employees; implicated by the media in insider trading fiascos or as the cause of the latest financial crisis; berated by politicians for earning excessive salaries and bonuses for the results produced; condemned by the public as a group that tolerates damning examples of blatant dishonesty, lack of integrity and self-aggrandizement.

I believe the blame for such a sorry state of affairs is twofold.

First, many in business conceive of management as a series of techniques to get results; hence the existence of flavour-of-the-month management fads. Second, many treat management as a launching pad to greater status. We should not be surprised that people on the front lines of a business often feel little loyalty to their company, buffeted as they are by change for change's sake and managers who are out for their personal gain.

No Clue About the Craft of Management

As a young manager, I reported to a regional GM who managed a retail division with 3,000+ employees. Business was tough and the politics of the division even tougher. It was not an easy time for any of us. However, the GM had a good team below him. We worked hard to implement the strategic plan and build sales. Our GM, however, added little value to our work. His idea of contributing was to empty garbage cans when he visited the stores, look continuously overwhelmed and "manage up," all the while sending us unsettling signals that implied we were responsible for the poor results.

The reality of our situation became clear to us during a meeting one day. We had been called together to review the results of the last quarter. The results were rough, but the team was reasonably buoyant – until our leader, looking harassed and dispirited, exclaimed in a loud voice, "This assignment is going to ruin my career!"

Talk about being able to cut the atmosphere with a knife. We all knew we were swimming on our own – that any hope of support and protection from our politicized masters in the future would be thrown aside as our GM frantically grabbed the first career life raft he could find. Any trust we had in him was destroyed. As a result, we focused on career survival, too, which, of course, distracted us from running the business.

The team hung together in the short term and then unravelled as team members left to find more fulfilling work. The division lost ground, morale plunged among employees and the implementation of the strategy failed. Many employees suffered.

The trouble was that our manager had no clue about the craft of management: the honour, discipline and mettle required to support those who work for the organization, by protecting and nurturing them and giving them honest feedback on their performance – and all this while demanding and getting extraordinary levels of performance from them.

Management Is a Craft

I believe management can recapture its mission as a noble profession that enables the economy, but only if it is treated as a craft.

Crafts are more than ways to earn income. As the workplace ethnographer Randy Hodson points out, they are lifetime commitments in which the work itself is intrinsically enjoyable and becomes an integral part of how the practitioners of the crafts see themselves.[2]

In medieval Europe, master craftsmen of particular professions organized into guilds. The guilds promoted the lifelong pursuit of mastery. To be elected to the guild as a master craftsman, aspirants had to pass through learning steps as apprentices progressing to journeymen, demonstrating discipline and a level of capability in the skills, knowledge and wisdom of the profession. Even when they had reached the apogee of their profession, these masters continued to hone their ability, as well as to expand and perfect their understanding of the craft.

Real CEO management is a craft, a vocation, a life's calling. At its very best, CEO management is even spiritual, for it unlocks the potential of people to work together, enabling them to create and achieve things they never dreamed possible. The craft of executive management is a highly effective means to get consistent, high productivity out of large groups of individuals, higher than they can achieve singly or even in small groups. Management at the CEO level is a messy business that requires self-sacrifice and humility in the service of others. Those who get it right can build dynamic, productive organizations that achieve great results through highly engaged employees.

The men and women who practice the craft of CEO management know they are involved not in "leadership over management" but in "managerial leadership." As McGill management professor Henry Mintzberg says, who would want to follow a manager who cannot lead, or a leader who cannot manage?[3]

For you as a CEO, management as a craft requires you to choose a framework – a set of processes, systems, skills and knowledge – that will enable you to engage large groups of employees with confidence, clarity and consistency. Having chosen a system, you will stick with it, modifying it minimally as you pursue mastery of your craft. You can become a lifelong student of a set of management principles that will enable you to be a superb manager, an expert in successfully leading and managing large groups of employees: 250 to 25,000+ of them.

So where does all this leave you?

As the chief executive of a corporation or head of a division in charge of more than 250+ employees, you represent probably the top .5% of the management profession. Being a member of this tiny group makes you special, if not unique. You now represent the profession of management and carry huge accountability and social responsibility. You have created your own company or have been entrusted with significant resources, including a significant number of employees, and are challenged to maximize the productivity of these resources in the pursuit of a strategy.

The influence of your actions goes far beyond your shareholders and customers. As a result of building a successful company, you affect the well-being and confidence of your employees. This in turn affects their families and the communities they live in, at times profoundly. Business author Ian McDonald tells of the effect the successful transformation of an aluminum smelter in New Zealand had on the community. According to the recollection of one of the project's principals, social services in the surrounding community saw a coincidental 30% drop in domestic violence reports. Unshackling the capability of the employees to do their best work transformed people at home.[4] Like the ripple caused by a stone dropped into a pond, the success of your company sends benefits out into the community, sometimes in ways you could not have imagined.

You have the opportunity to create something prosperous for your shareholders and beneficial to the community in which your company works. How have you been prepared to do this? How do you convert a detached, disengaged workforce into one that is highly engaged, innovative, proprietorial, effective and efficient in whatever work it has to accomplish, one that no longer says, "Thank God it's Friday!" but "I can't wait for Monday!"

Pick a Model – but Choose Wisely

A message you will encounter throughout this book is that employees require consistency and clarity in what they are expected to do. CEOs who do not practice the craft of management fall into the trap of implementing haphazard initiatives that are not thought through and integrated into the overall organization's structure and management and accountability processes. They kick these initiatives off with great fanfare and then watch them atrophy and die because the organization's systems are unable to support them.

These baseless change initiatives just create confusion and pain. Employees dismiss them as fads that caught the fancy of a fickle executive. To them it is BOHICA (Bend Over, Here It Comes Again!), yet another distraction to keep them from creating value. "How many times are you going to restructure the company?" they ask. "Please leave us alone," they beg. This is where Dilbert gets all his wonderful examples of ludicrous policies that unwitting CEOs inflict on their employees.

You have to select the model with which you will manage. Choose one methodology, believe in it, then practice and develop deep expertise in it. Work with it for the rest of your life. But be careful. You need to choose something beyond the latest management fad, lest the model you choose makes you look like all of the other inept CEOs who perpetrate ill-considered processes and policies on their employees.

Your model should allow you and your managers to talk about the profession of management proudly and cogently. Are you able to do this? I am sure you can talk about your work, but can you frame your work clearly, referencing a set of organizational and management methodologies and practices? You need to understand the "whole organizational system" and the set of CEO management principles required to manage it.

Yes, you are distracted by a myriad of legitimate issues: your board, investors, regulators, clients, strategy and quarterly results – the cries for your attention are endless. But you can never afford to lose sight of your long-term intent to create the best organization you possibly can to deliver great results.

A well-run company is a hierarchy of capability. The person at the top of the organization – you! – should have the highest capability and skills, and so be able to add value to the work of everyone else in your organization. Your challenge is to manage. You must become the organization's manager, able to assess and tend to your organization's stresses and strains, rightly judging the load your organization can bear without collapsing. You need to know the craft of CEO management.

Your Challenge

You have to dare to be the greatest CEO you can be, or you should not take the job. You have a choice to be a good CEO and do what good CEOs do, or be negligent and fake it. You are expected to raise the performance of your company.

You believe that employees are important. But when you make that statement, do you actually believe it to be true? Are you as centric to your employees, especially the front line, as you could be? You want to achieve great results. You will do so if your employees feel useful at work and are engaged. Employee engagement does not come solely from greater pay or other material considerations; it comes when they believe they are contributing to producing something that is good.

CEOs have an incredible impact on their organizations, often without realizing it. CEOs create the working environment throughout the organization, by personal example and behaviour, and by how they manage. The effectiveness of each and every individual in the organization, top to bottom, is affected, for better or worse, by the management systems the CEO puts in place. The only question for you, the CEO, is: Are you going to deliberately and consciously put in place systems that promote an environment in which every employee does his or her best work? Or are you going to make these decisions by default? If you fail to consciously create a high-performance environment, you, in effect, choose to allow the organization to stumble along with a grossly sub-optimal strategy. This is both immoral and self-defeating. Immoral, because you are wasting shareholder money, squandering social equity and creating a workplace that is demeaning to your employees, customers and vendors. And self-defeating, because ultimately this will cost you your job.

How many CEOs care about this? A good minority do, but many others are preoccupied with their own ego and importance and see their assignment just as another job to be done.

What about you? It is great to say you value people and results, but if you don't understand what to do and then do something about it, it is just words. This is where this book comes in. I believe that once you understand what you have to do, you will take it very seriously, actually do it and enjoy it immensely.

Get Practices That Work

As a CEO who practices the craft of CEO management, you will understand how to use practices that will guide and control your company. You will set clear, strategic destinations that your organization can then achieve. You will create competitive agility and advantage through knowing what has to be put in place to achieve it. You will ensure that expert knowledge and advice of your management and front-line employees are communicated back up the organization and the strategic intent from the top is thereby adjusted and cascaded down. You will ensure that the layers of the organization add value to the work to be done rather than destroy or distort it. You will exert consistent control because you know the practices you're working with and the results that come from using them.

The effort you put into mastering your craft will give you insights into opportunities that were elusive or invisible to you before. You will be able to balance the needs of your business more surely and effectively. Your employees will be freed from having to guess at goals.

The result? Employees get to do great work, and you feel in control of it. Everyone gains clarity: employees know what is expected and are set free to do it. Your managers add real value to their work, becoming coaches as well as cops. Coming to work is fun!

Executives' Poor Reputation

According to Canadian compensation expert Mark Van Clieaf, in an article in the *Ivey Business Journal,* instead of focusing on the high-level strategic work for which they get paid, many executive managers spend their time doing operational work that should be the purview of employees at lower (and much cheaper) levels, to the detriment of long-term value for both the shareholder and the organization. Much of this pressure comes from ill-conceived shareholder movements.[5] A 2006 survey of CFOs by academics John R. Graham, Campbell R. Harvey and Shiva Rajgopal found that over half of these executives would sacrifice projects that, with positive net present value (NPV), would help them make their quarterly numbers.[6]

Nor, according to their employees, are executives doing a very good job. For all our talk about leadership, we aren't really leading people. A national survey by the Canadian Management Centre and Ipsos Reid in 2012 found that 61% of employees don't trust what senior managers say, and less than 40% feel that senior managers communicate well what is happening. Worse, less than half believed that senior managers provided a clear vision for their work or had confidence in their decisions.[7]

Is this why Canadians consider chief executives to be even less trustworthy than lawyers or taxi drivers, according to another 2012 Ipsos Reid poll, for Postmedia News and Global Television?[8] Taking into account attributes like integrity, reliability and commitment to promises, less than 20% of Canadians polled said that they would trust CEOs.

Not all of their distrust is misplaced. Although as an executive leadership consultant for the last twenty-five years (after being a line manager for twenty years prior to that), I have been privileged to work with some incredible managers and seen the best of the profession. I have also seen a lot of the worst. I have even wished that a certain senior manager could be disbarred from the profession due to gross misconduct.

Such value-destroyers are fired only to pop up somewhere else and continue their destructive behaviours. Sometimes the problems they cause are papered over, and their company quietly transfers them to another "diocese" to begin their malfeasance anew, similar to the way the Roman Catholic Church handled its errant priests. This is an example of the abdication of management accountability – an inability to manage effectively in the face of highly sensitive and corrupt behaviours. Only now is the Church being forced to take stock. Will the pope eventually step up to his accountabilities to rebuild the reputation of his organization?

All this distrust is affecting employees' productivity and company profitability because trust and engagement are linked. BlessingWhite found in an international survey that engaged employees were much more likely to trust both their own manager and senior management.[9] Yet, according to a Towers Watson survey in 2012, only a third of Canadian employees are "sustainably engaged"; employers pay dearly for the results: high percentages of absenteeism, low rates of retention and decreased levels of productivity.[10] Greater distrust reduces the effectiveness of employees in negotiating their work with one another. Cross-functional work suffers because more has to be specifically stated. When front-line employees distrust management, they develop an "it's not my job" mentality, to stay out of trouble. Problems that lower levels could resolve either must be escalated to ever-higher levels of management (pulling managers down into operational work and driving out trust and profits) or be left to fester unresolved.

The net effect is the continued undermining of the great institution of management. CEOs are going to replace lawyers in jokes if this free fall continues.

"What's the definition of tragedy?"

"A busload of CEOs going over a cliff with one empty seat!"

One shudders.

It's Your Job, Not HR's

If you are like most managers, you are probably thinking that what I am discussing in this chapter is work for Human Resources, not you, the CEO. "This touchy-feely stuff is best left to the 'people people' down in HR," you may be saying to yourself.

I am afraid this is not so! This is your work, not HR's. It is CEO management work. You, not HR, sit at the top of your organization. You have the most power; you are the senior manager. The board holds you, not HR, accountable to create the strategy for your division or company. You make it all happen by choosing the top team, defining the company's work and priorities and organizing the work across functions. You and your managers manage; HR supports.

Since you are the most capable member of your organization to do this work (if you aren't, why are you in this role?), you are the person with the maximum overview and understanding of how your strategy can be translated into operating plans and implemented by the hundreds of employees you manage. You are the one who can see most clearly how constructing an organization that effectively implements your strategy and runs smoothly will create the results you are determined to achieve. Therefore, your ability to effectively manage the pain of your company truly matters to all your employees and warrants your time and attention. HR is there to support you.

Jos Decides to Learn

Jos Wintermans, the CEO introduced to you earlier, didn't stay despondent in his early days as CEO. He looked at his situation and took charge of his destiny.

"I decided I had to go and learn how to do this," he says.

And learn he did: the company he managed became a spectacular success, with output increasing twofold and profitability fivefold. Wintermans went on to successfully lead other companies, such as building supplier Sodisco-Howden and medical testing company LifeLabs. The CEO management principles he left in place at CTAL were adhered to by the next four CEOs, providing employees of the company with the consistency and clarity they needed to do great work. I had the privilege of working with them all. Of course, the CEOs who followed brought their own style and management preferences to their work. But none of them set out to deconstruct what Wintermans had created.

Ensuring Gain by Stopping the Pain

I am always stunned that poorly run companies, ones in which employees are disrespected and mistreated, survive. Presumably these employees must feel it is OK to work there or have no alternatives. Pop the hood of these companies and you will see a lot of enduring dysfunction and pain, but the employees have become so inured to it, so habituated to the situation, they just don't care anymore. The CEOs of such companies become accustomed to the status quo, too. They don't understand what to do about what they face, or they ignore the reality of what is happening.

But of course we are not talking about you, the reader! What I am saying is that, now that you have taken this job as CEO, the status quo is not good enough for you – it's unacceptable. To change things, however, you need to become aware of your organization's pain and who or what causes it.

One of your core accountabilities as a CEO who practices the craft of management is to create an environment in which all employees can do their best work: it is of vital importance for you to always think of the total number of employees in your organization. Another, related core CEO accountability is to aim to leave the organization stronger than you found it.

In your role managing hundreds of employees, you need to develop a heightened awareness of the pain you and your employees experience. You need to be able to identify and solve what causes them pain and frustration and limits their productivity.

Routinely in my work with the C-suite over the past twenty-five years, I have seen symptoms in company after company that point to deeper management and accountability problems. These pains hinder, or at their worst block, hundreds of employees from working efficiently and effectively on implementing their CEO's strategy. Your management accountability as CEO is to remove these blockers to enable all of your employees to do the work your managers delegate to them. You must learn to do it for hundreds or thousands of your employees. You are now managing on a completely different scale, as a master of the craft of management. When you visit the doctor's office, you describe the pain you're experiencing. The doctor diagnoses the symptoms. This is what you need to be able to do, vis-à-vis your organization, if you are going to effectively manage hundreds or thousands of employees. You need to be able to describe your own pain at your level. This pain will represent key corporate malaise and blockers that threaten to keep you from achieving your strategy.

The Pain List

The Pain List shows some of the most typical CEO pain points. Some are strategic in nature and can cripple effectiveness if not addressed. Others are interdependent and arise from related root causes. All of them are solvable if you decide to stop being just half a CEO. If you dare to learn the other half of management, they are just symptoms of organizational debilitation that can be set right. In engaging to solve them, you are taking the first step in managing your organization.

Take a look at the following list and tick off the pains that resonate with you. Whatever affects you will be worse for hundreds of your employees, and will compromise their performance.

My customers get average service
☐ We seem to accept the average service we sometimes give our customers
☐ The organization could or should care more about its customers

☐	I am afraid the organization does not have the capability to meet the higher demands of our customers in the future
☐	We need to transform our attitude or behaviour towards our customers
☐	If we are not careful, our competitors will "eat our lunch"!
☐	We have three years to get our value offering right. Otherwise, we die
We cannot create our strategy	
☐	I cannot work with my direct reports to create the strategy I require. Some of them cannot grasp the concepts
☐	My executive cannot translate the company strategy into meaningful functional strategy for their teams
☐	Employees throughout my organization do not understand how their work fits the strategy
☐	If my company wanted to acquire another company, I am not sure we would have robust enough structure, processes, systems and management capability to effectively absorb and integrate it into our organization
My management team does not deliver and does not exude confidence	
☐	For the money I pay my management team, I do not get enough value in return
☐	Nobody wants to offend anybody else
☐	We never get to the heart of what matters
☐	I keep getting surprises
☐	Managers don't hold their direct reports accountable for their output
☐	Executives are always bickering about interdepartmental handoffs

☐	Executives don't apprise each other of their work
☐	Executives constantly take end-runs around each other
☐	Too many managers have their own agendas, which undermine the implementation of the company's strategy
☐	Executives do not passionately focus on the productivity and welfare of our front-line employees
☐	Managers are uncomfortable making decisions and prefer to avoid them – especially high-profile ones
☐	Managers do not manage consistently
☐	Managers won't make the tough, uncomfortable decisions that would substantially advance the business
☐	Executives do not prioritize and integrate the work of the organization to manage employee workload
☐	Managers are not proud to be managers
☐	Managers do not work hard and effectively
I cannot get the things done that I want	
☐	I keep getting surprises
☐	Major projects are delayed and come in late and over budget
☐	My managers don't speak up when they get into trouble in their work. Nobody is going to say that the work is going to come in late, much less that it will not work as effectively and efficiently as originally planned
☐	I keep hearing we have 80% to 90% of the facts to make a decision, but we never get that last 10% to 20% and actually make a decision
☐	Large, interdependent processes designed to engage/service customers are costly and inefficient, mired down in turf wars

☐	We simply don't make decisions fast enough. We get stuck in "analysis paralysis"
☐	Employees are bogged down in meetings that often have 15+ people in them
☐	Nobody says no to more work. The culture influences people to accept it quietly, despite there being little chance of getting it done
Employee morale and engagement are low; employees:	
☐	Do not care
☐	Do not understand how their work fits into the strategy
☐	Do not respect their managers
☐	Are preoccupied with the importance of titles
☐	Have acrimonious relationships with employees from other functions
☐	Do not see a future at the company
☐	Do not feel fairly paid
☐	Do not feel listened to
☐	Do the work they believe is important, not the work that will advance my strategy

In conclusion, allow me to say something very serious to you: Don't dare take the job of CEO and just sit in a fancy chair and preen your feathers. Do something with this opportunity. Being a great CEO is hard work. But success in this great role is within your grasp. You can close your skill gap as a CEO by learning and mastering the seven CEO management principles, the focus of the next part of this book.

Executive Summary

1. Management is the omnipresent profession of our society.

2. Reputationally, CEOs are in trouble.

3. The craft of executive management is not understood or valued. When it *is* recognized, it is often implemented inconsistently.

4. As a CEO, you need to be known for your integrity in how you engage and manage large groups of employees.

5. You achieve this by choosing to learn a framework, a system of principles, practices and policies that comprise a way to manage a whole company of employees. You need to stick to this methodology and practice the craft for the rest of your career in order to become an expert.

6. As a CEO you are given a unique opportunity in life. You are a rare part of the population that is fortunate to have such a large amount of resources to make a big impact on the world. Seize the opportunity to do something great.

7. You need to become adept at recognizing and curing the pain in your organization that prevents your employees from doing their best work and inherently weakens your organization.

PART TWO

Closing the Gap

Introduction to Part Two

Seven principles make up the craft of CEO management, and, in what follows, I devote a chapter to each one of them. They are:

- Principle #1: Create Your Strategy
- Principle #2: Choose Your Organization's Functional Structure
- Principle #3: Level the Organization
- Principle #4: Define the Work
- Principle #5: Manage Your Organization's Lateral Relationships
- Principle #6: Build the Required Talent
- Principle #7: Make It All Happen with Effective Management

Each of these chapters includes a confrontational "how dare you" statement and illustrates it with an example culled from my twenty-five years of consultative practice. I follow that with a general discussion of the principle, demonstrating the benefits that it can achieve in your organization and the pains it can solve. I end each chapter with Action Steps, which include reflective questions meant to help you assess where you are with the principle, and an Executive Summary.

Each principle is a valuable tool on its own. And when the principles are implemented together, they raise employee productivity and engagement and create true organizational energy, efficiency and effectiveness. The result? Delighted workers, delighted customers and delighted shareholders.

The seven CEO management principles are based on my years of consulting work with CEOs such as Jos Wintermans, introduced to you at the beginning of this book, and the influence of the ideas of a researcher he introduced me to: Elliott Jaques.

You may not have heard of the late Dr. Jaques, but he is increasingly known among some of the world's most successful companies. Deloitte's Michael E. Raynor, co-author with Clayton M. Christensen of the bestselling *The Innovator's Solution*,[11] calls him "the most undeservedly ignored management researcher of the modern era."

He used Jaques' theory of requisite organization as the basis of his 2005 book *The Strategy Paradox*.[12]

Jaques' management theories were founded on over fifty years of extensive studies at organizations across the world led by him, his many consulting colleagues and industry managers such as Warren Kinston and Ralph Rowbottom with Britain's National Health Service,[13] David Billis at Tata Sons,[14] Ian Macdonald and Catherine Burke at the international mining company CRA,[15] Stephen Clement and Maurice Dutrisac at Whirlpool Canada,[16] Brian Dive at Unilever and Tesco[17] and many others.

Jaques met with Jos Wintermans, George Harding, Carlos Rigby and Wintermans' employees at Canadian Tire Acceptance, which was where and when I first met him.

These are not pie-in-the-sky concepts that never see real-world application. Jaques began this work when he was engaged by the late Lord Wilfred Brown, CEO of Glacier Metal Company in the UK, to help him create a better, more profitable company. Famed management expert Peter Drucker called Jaques' twenty-five years at Glacier with Brown "the most extensive study of actual worker behavior in large-scale industry."[18]

The seven CEO management principles are my distillation of Jaques' philosophy. In figure 6, they fill the top half of the diagram. Of course, you must retain the management practices at the bottom of the hourglass to manage your direct reports, but to be more than half a CEO, to be capable of effectively managing hundreds of employees – the whole of your organization – you must master the seven CEO management principles.

These principles are not an exhaustive list of everything you need, but they are the core of what you need to become an effective CEO. Implementing a complex strategy for a large organization will require you to break apart the work and place each piece at the right level in the organization. You must be able to manage the work of your organization like an orchestra conductor who takes highly capable musicians and aligns and integrates their skills to produce a unique performance.

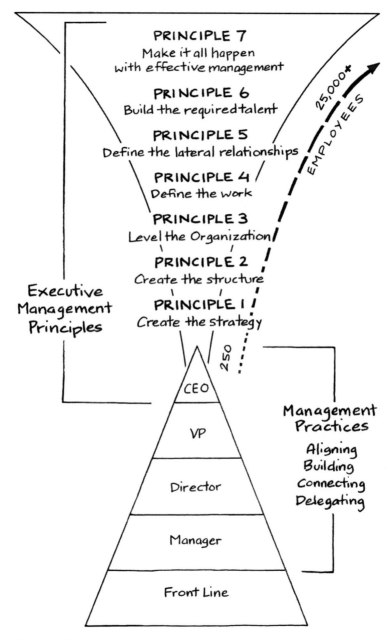

Figure 6: The complete CEO.

CHAPTER FOUR

CEO Management Principle #1: Create Your Strategy

Jos Wintermans could have been forgiven for thinking, when he became president of Canadian Tire's credit card subsidiary in 1988, that the corporate strategy of Canadian Tire Acceptance was sound. The company had just had a pretty good year. But Wintermans could see that the market was changing – that CTAL could no longer maintain the 28.8% interest rate charged on overdue amounts. It was like an opium habit, a highly lucrative but unreasonable charge to customers that was simply not sustainable.

CTAL could not continue to count on this one trick that it had up its sleeve. Instead, in 1989, the organization decided to obtain a licence with MasterCard. Visa was out of reach; it was owned by the big banks, which were unwilling to grant a licence. CTAL had tried to purchase Enroute, without success. MasterCard was the company's best strategic opportunity. It took four long years to obtain the licence, but what a change when that finally happened. The old Canadian Tire card had been accepted only at Canadian Tire, whereas the new one was accepted everywhere. Over time, the entire original Canadian Tire portfolio was converted to MasterCard and charges on the card reduced by over ten percentage points.

Wintermans had it right: everything starts with strategy. In fact, the six other principles of the CEO's craft rely on a clear, developed and coherent strategy to succeed. Strategy drives everything.

The CEO's craft involves meeting profit targets, but all the while developing long-term shareholder value. If you do not take care of the longer-term goals for your company, the markets and fate will take care of them for you. They are not kind mistresses. People who rely on them instead of their intelligence don't last long at the top.

How dare you manage your company without describing a clear future!

In their book *Exploring Corporate Strategy*, Gerry Johnson and Kevan Scholes define strategy as follows: "Strategy is the direction and scope of an organisation over the long-term, which achieves *advantage* for the organisation through its configuration of *resources and competencies* within a challenging *environment* to meet the needs of the market and to fulfill *stakeholder* expectations."[19] Strategy gives order and focus to the work of your organization. When you make it clear, you can engage all your employees in the purpose of the company; you can create energy and proprietorship in doing something worthwhile.

The first step in determining your strategy is to create mission and vision statements. To create a strategic plan, you need to be clear, before you start planning, about "who we are" and "what we aspire to be." The two statements set the context for everything you will do as a company.

I define a mission and a vision statement as follows:

- *Mission statement*: A description of what the company does. Do not embellish it with lofty statements; try to keep it succinct, focused and contained in two sentences. What is not said or included in a mission statement is as important as what is said. Mission statements define what we "will" and "will not do." Therefore they should focus on the strategy and work of the company and on preventing breakaway initiatives that would undermine the strategy
- *Vision statement*: A lofty aspirational statement that pulls the company forward. This statement indicates something to work towards. Again, keep it simple – preferably one sentence long

Even if your company is in flux and you feel you cannot develop a vision statement at this time, your job is to see past the immediate problems and continue to build towards a longer-term future for the company. This is how you add value as a CEO. You must focus on being a strategist and manager of hundreds or thousands of employees.

Let's look at sample mission and vision statements, using a fictitious company, Banda Builders. This company has been in the construction business for fifteen years and has grown steadily to the point that it now has 400 employees. It specializes in multiple-dwelling developments. Its mission statement is:

We deliver houses to discerning clients who are looking for well-designed, well-made, healthy and environmentally responsible homes at a reasonable price.

Its vision statement is:

To perfect the art and science of building by creating beautiful, healthy, sustainable homes – redefining the way houses are built.

Neither the mission nor the vision statement should refer to profit or shareholder value. Profits and shareholder value are the *result* of delivering the vision. They are both products of a well-run business. Nothing will work in the long term if the purpose of a company is defined around money. This type of preferred future will not engage your employees. Most want to be part of something bigger and nobler than just wealth or profit creation.

Once you've articulated "here's what we do" and "here's what we aspire to be," it's time for you to address the fundamental question of strategy, "How do we survive and thrive in a competitive landscape?" All organizations operate in a competitive landscape. They all compete for the resources that are required for sustainable success. Strategy is the decision on what the company needs to excel at in order to accomplish the vision. It must mesh with vision, available resources and environmental conditions (markets, competitors, suppliers, technology, environment and so on).

To determine how you will survive and thrive in a competitive landscape, you need to answer six sub-questions. Banda Builders' answers are shown after each question.

Where will we choose to compete? What markets do we choose to be in, and with what products?

- We want to build 500 houses per year
- We choose to compete in the mass market, not in the bespoke house market
- We build in Southern Ontario with a view to expanding elsewhere

How will we win? Why will customers choose us and not someone else? What is our competitive edge?

- A key strategy is to match the price points of conventional houses of equivalent size, features and finish. We will lose business if we cannot match price points. Given that, we intend to win business through significant health and energy benefits and through superior design
- With regard to developers, we will also win business by providing a sixty-day house. Reducing the time to build provides substantial reductions in requirements for working capital

How will we know we have won? What are the measurements of success and irrefutable results we will achieve?

- We want to be the company to beat in our sector
- We are growing the business to a capacity of 500+ homes per year
- We are growing revenue to $100 million per year
- We deliver development houses in sixty days from confirmed order to handing over the keys

What capabilities do we need to win?

We must be exceptionally good at:

- Design: our houses must be attractive aesthetically as well as functionally
- Engineering: good engineering ensures that components

built at different locations fit together properly when
assembled on-site for optimal energy performance
- Production management: managing the production workflow
  delivers a steady stream of houses, on time, on budget
  and with the necessary quality
- Relationship management: developing and mastering
  productive relationships with developers is critical to
  our success
- Marketing: we must maintain and increase our reputation
  as builders of unique, healthy, quality homes

What systems do we need?

- We need to track the health performance of our homes
  so we can demonstrate our capabilities to potential buyers
- We need excellent systems for cost management
- We need to stay on top of what home buyers are looking for
  so we can continue to offer houses that are current, fresh
  and appealing

**How will we organize ourselves to successfully execute our
chosen strategy?**

- We will follow the seven CEO management principles

The essential point? Developing strategy involves making choices.
It's often as important to say what you will not do as what you will. By
making choices, you decide how you're going to win the competitive
game in front of you. By making choices, you can focus your resources
on the areas that really matter. By making choices, you can make your
strategy crystal clear. Fail to make these choices and you commit your
organization to mediocrity – and ultimately to failure.

As Michael Raynor points out in his book *The Strategy Paradox,*[20]
managing at the executive level involves managing strategic uncertainty: balancing a portfolio of options because you cannot know
whether a strategy will succeed even if everyone executes perfectly.
Lower levels don't have strategic uncertainty; they focus on executing

the strategy and getting concrete things done. Remember, however, that managing strategic uncertainty must be rooted in the realities on the front line. Knowing your business is key to managing uncertainty.

Strategy requires data and analysis, but, as Henry Mintzberg states, more importantly, it requires thinking.[21] Strategic thinking should not be confused with strategic planning. The former is a combination of intuition and distinguishing and synthesizing abstract strands and trends to perceive an integrated perspective of the challenges facing the organization and where it should be heading.

Your Executive Team

Strategic planning is not a solitary activity. It is not something you hand down to the organization. Your executive team needs to be part of the process of developing strategy. Your role is to manage the process so every member of the team has a legitimate opportunity to influence the final result, by giving you their best advice, while you retain the final decision-making authority. If the members of your executive team cannot do strategic work, they have been promoted farther than they should have been. You need to remove them from their role. They cannot remain on your team, because they cannot contribute value to your main priority: the process of enabling the company to succeed.

There are three main reasons for engaging your team.

First, you need their full commitment to the result, and that commitment will come only through engagement.

Second, you will be holding each of them accountable for implementing the strategy within their functions; full engagement means they will be far better equipped to translate corporate strategy into functional strategy.

Third, you need their functional expertise and perspective to ensure that the strategy takes account of specific functional issues. Working with the top team leads to a better strategy. Without their input, your strategy will probably falter, stall or even fail. Why? Because your managers will not help their employees understand the strategy, and therefore will not be able to support it.

I have already used the word "accountability" several times in this book, and it will crop up many times right to the end. There is a crucial distinction between "accountability" and "responsibility":

- **Accountability** is a contract between managers and their direct reports. Through dialogue (see page 52), the manager states: "You have agreed to accept this task and to complete it and to tell me when you know you cannot. I will hold you to account to deliver it as we agreed"
- **Responsibility** is a feeling of obligation and caring, which, if it is not tied to accountability, can end at the level of feeling; in other words, it may or may not lead to action, and when it does, it is likely to be misdirected or uncoordinated in terms of your strategy. It can lead highly conscientious and motivated individuals to emerge as white knights tilting at the wrong windmills

Responsibility without accountability in an organization is a recipe for undermining the implementation of strategic work. It can drain an organization of valuable resources because they are put into the service of breakaway initiatives that are not on strategy.

As CEO, you reinforce the organization's accountability to your strategy by working with your executive team to create effective and productive working relationships between managers and their direct report managers. The accountabilities thus contracted are critical to the success of your company. This process ensures that work gets done and gets done well.

You are accountable for the enterprise strategy, but you can succeed only if the strategy provides managers and employees with an enablement vehicle for their own unarticulated visions.[22] They get on board not when you coerce them, but when you help them do great work. For your strategy to succeed, your executive team must coalesce around it.

Creating the strategy is one thing; engaging your team in the development of the strategy is another. As one CEO told me, unless you are all joined at the hip, it's not going to happen. Your strategy has to become the team's strategy, too. For this to happen, you must develop the strategy in dialogue with them. Note that leaders who focus on inspiring great work are not as successful as those who focus on helping their employees achieve the great work that some of them already want to accomplish.

Dialogue and Best Advice

Dialogue is a two-way conversation with your direct reports, essential to soliciting their views and best advice. Done effectively, it builds relationships marked by trust and respect.

All employees are accountable to give their managers their **best advice**. Best advice is their opinion about work they are doing for their manager, or their views on any work their manager is engaged in to help him or her make the best decisions possible. Managers do not have to agree with the best advice they receive, but if they decline it, they should explain why.

Together, dialogue and best advice are critical to creating and clarifying strategy.

- Successful CEOs have sufficient confidence and character to welcome best advice, as it often provides them with information they wish they did not have to hear – but are grateful they did!
- Failing CEOs cannot or will not listen to information or advice that contradicts their poor assumptions, beliefs or plans

---

Implement Functional Strategy Cascades

Once you and your team decide on the strategy, disaggregate it into well-aligned strategies for each function of the organization. By "disaggregate" I mean unbundle, pick apart, break into smaller pieces. Your executives need to be able to translate their strategies into plans that their own team can understand.

Here's how this happens.

The functional heads engage their team by cascading the strategy down through the organization, level by level. The key to success is to ensure that dialogue and best advice occur freely. I refer to this process as "washing" the strategy with employees. Through this process, they get to understand their part of the strategy while telling you and your managers what will and will not work. Best advice is critical to the success of the plan. It enables you to make the best decisions possible. Managers at all levels – including you, at the very top – need best advice.

Through this cascade, your strategic objectives are translated from functional business plans to operational plans to implementation plans that are then executed by front-line employees. (See figure 7.)

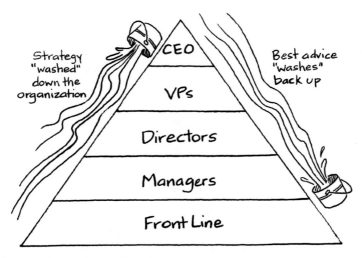

Figure 7: Strategy cascading down your organization.

The Key Output: Alignment

Through the cascade process, the members of your team obtain answers to the issues that confront them in terms of implementing the strategy. The challenge for you, the CEO, is to ensure that they have all of the same answers. They cannot work effectively together if they have developed a different set of answers to those developed by their neighbour in the next office. Alignment is a critical challenge in achieving success.

You and your executive team must work together to integrate the work of your organization. Your executives must put aside the independent, tribal instincts of their function and integrate its needs into what gets the enterprise closer to achieving its strategic visionary goal. Executives must look out for the health and welfare of the whole enterprise, not just their own function.

Your role as CEO requires you to engage your senior team in a strategic dialogue that concludes with a plan around which every executive team member can unite. Their roles require them to do the thinking necessary to translate that plan into a strategy and plans for their function. The strategic process is both top-down and bottom-up, and it is always done in dialogue. This process may take time to hash out together. The strategy should provide employees with a way to articulate their desires. An uncertain strategy, communicated and cascaded uncertainly, creates uncertainty – and that translates into employee resistance, not support.

A Word of Caution When Building Strategy

I have found that, early in an assignment, CEOs can inherit team members who disagree with them because of personal animosity or strategic direction. This often manifests itself not as direct conflict but as subtle, passive-aggressive resistance – what could be called "malicious compliance." These enemies will often sound appeasing in meetings, then work to undermine the CEO in private conversations with their peers and direct reports. In the worst cases, these employees will do an end-run around the CEO and take their case directly to friends on the board.

Figure 8 shows the quandary that you as CEO will face. The longer you leave visceral non-supporters in place, the more powerful they can become, especially if your strategy starts to falter or other issues arise that can be seen to compromise your effectiveness. I have seen CEOs who have not dealt with this matter neutered and usurped, losing their jobs within twenty-four months. Apart from the personal pain you will feel, the major cost of inaction is the confusion, instead of a clear understanding and acceptance of your strategic plan, that cascades throughout your company.

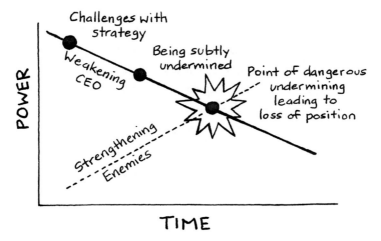

Figure 8: Watch out that your enemies do not undermine you.

You may be hesitant to fire these people. What will get you over the hump is realizing that leaving people on the team who work against the strategic direction blocks your employees' productivity. It is nigh unto impossible to work effectively with a disenchanted senior manager. Time and time again, I have heard CEOs who failed to move such managers out speak not only of their regrets but also of the massive added pain and risk they took on as a result.

Do not avoid addressing those who oppose the new direction. Otherwise, they will become enemies. Fire them before they fire you!

A great way to understand which managers are your supporters and which your enemies is to classify them into one of the following categories:

- "Family": they will support you, no matter what
- Friends: they will support you, up to a point (after which they will abandon you)
- Fence-sitters: they will wait to see which way the wind is blowing before declaring themselves

- Foes: they will fight you, up to a point (after which they will concede)
- Fiends: they will fight you no matter what

At the extremes of this spectrum are:

- Family, who will support you, no matter what – so look after them, but don't worry too much about their loyalty
- Fiends, who will fight you, no matter what – so either move them out of the organization, or find a way to neutralize their opposition; don't waste time trying to convert them

Having dealt with fiends, you can do a cold-blooded assessment of how to retain your friends, how to convert some fence-sitters (preferably the more influential ones) to become friends and how to get some foes (again, preferably the more influential ones) to at least sit on the fence. At the end of the day, you do not need to convert everyone; you need a critical mass of support, enough to carry the organization with you.

The Critical Necessity of a Clear Strategy

When Jos Wintermans started the strategic planning process with the existing executive team at Canadian Tire Acceptance, he was aware of the challenge he had on his hands. Some team members thought of it as irrelevant work that distracted them from "real" operations work. Some were too individualistic to work effectively with other team members. Some simply could not do the type of thinking necessary to translate the enterprise strategy into shorter-term functional objectives for their own team. None of them was used to the debate and teamwork that are the operating system of an effective executive team.

Wintermans knew he had to build the team up. He created a culture of best advice, coached some into collaborating with their peers and fired those who could not or would not do the real work of the executive.

It paid off. When, eight years later, he left CTAL for a job on the executive of the parent company, Wintermans had created a strategy that permeated everything the employees did. You could step into the call centre in Welland, Ontario, and customer service representatives could tell you how what they did tied into the company's overall strategy. That consistency had grown CTAL from 650 to 1,400 employees and allowed them to create competitive advantages like becoming the world's first non-bank to issue a private label credit card. Clearly, Wintermans understood strategy to be the job of the chief executive.

The reason that creating strategy, the first of the seven CEO management principles, is so critical, is that it becomes the context and driving force for everything else. The rest of the principles enable you to implement, execute and achieve your strategy through the aligned and concerted work of hundreds of your employees.

Every part of your organization takes its cue from the strategy, aligning itself in service to its achievement. The following chapters in this part of the book explore the six remaining CEO management principles that will enable you to do this.

Action Steps

1. Do you have clear mission and vision statements? If not, you need to create them. Follow the definitions on pages 46–47 and create draft statements for discussion and refinement. These statements will give you context for everything you do.

2. With these statements in hand, review the following questions:
    a. Are they current?
    b. Do they provide clear context/relevance to you as you guide and manage the company?
    c. Can employees understand them when they read them?
    d. Are you clear what they exclude or prevent the company from doing?

3. Then answer the six fundamental sub-questions:
    a. Where will we choose to compete? What markets do we choose to be in, and with what products?

b. How will we win? Why will customers choose us and not someone else? What is our competitive edge?

c. How will we know we have won? What are the measurements of success and irrefutable results we will achieve?

d. What capabilities do we need to win?

e. What systems do we need?

f. How will we organize ourselves to successfully execute our chosen strategies?

4. Assess your top team. Is everyone on board? If not, take corrective action.

Executive Summary

1. Create mission and vision statements, because they will set context for all your employees regarding what their company does and what it aspires to become.

2. Your strategy frames the work of your organization and provides context for all of the work your managers and employees are held accountable to do.

3. Without strategy, you have an organization without purpose.

4. Without strategy, you cannot hold your employees accountable for their work.

5. Your executive team must be capable of translating your enterprise strategy into functional strategies.

CHAPTER FIVE

CEO Management Principle #2: Choose Your Organization's Functional Structure

Once, while working with a company, I observed an argument that developed at the executive level whether Call Centres or Marketing should specify the level of service that customers were to receive when speaking to call centre operators.

When passionate feelings erupted, with each division claiming priority, the CEO intervened, clearly and forcefully giving the accountability to Marketing.

Explaining her decision to me later, she said, "I hold Marketing accountable to develop our products, establish service levels and set profitability for each of our products. I hold our call centres accountable to provide excellent service at an excellent cost – a service level specified and contracted to the call centres by Marketing."

Next, she dealt with the initial questions and challenges that flowed from her decision. Opposition declined as she repeated her expectations. Things settled down, and the two divisions started to work efficiently together.

What did the CEO do here? She took the step of prioritizing her functional structure. She clarified that Marketing was the core function of the organization. She expected the call centres to provide services as specified. They did. And that drove positive results.

How dare you manage your company without creating a clear structure!

Structure is essential for teamwork. No professional sports team would compete if the players did not know their specific role. Structure is your organization's system of accountability and authority. It manifests as policy, roles and role relationships. It is how accountability for work is defined and distributed.

Structure is built by asking and answering these questions:

1. What functions are required to implement the strategy? (principle #2)

2. What functions report to the CEO? (principle #2)

3. What is the core function of the organization? (principle #2)

4. How many levels of management and employee work are required to implement the strategy? (principle #3)

5. What are the work roles, accountabilities and authorities required to implement the strategy? (principles #4 and #5)

6. What are the policies within which all employees will work? (principle #7)

Taken together, these elements comprise the structure within which your employees get their work done.

Choosing the Required Structure

With your strategy in hand (principle #1), you need to choose the required structure to implement it (principle #2).

Your organization should be structured so it enables ever-increasing performance and effectiveness in the achievement of your strategic goals. Sadly, most of the organizations I encounter aren't structured in this way. The CEO often appears woefully ignorant of the importance of aligned structure and how it affects employee behaviour and future corporate performance.

The board holds the CEO accountable for achieving strategic objectives. However, as CEO, you cannot do all of the work yourself – that's why there's an organization for you to lead. So as CEO you have to disaggregate your accountability for executing strategy into smaller chunks. You should structure this disaggregation as closely as possible to the organization's strategic objectives.

As a master who practices the craft of management, you build your organization to achieve the enterprise strategy. As Alfred Chandler first put it, over half a century ago, structure follows strategy.[23] To achieve your strategic goals, your entire organization must be focused and aligned on achieving them – putting all the wood behind the arrowhead. Your organization must be intentionally structured to achieve the purpose. As a master of the craft of CEO management, you do not delegate this work: creating the structure is your management work; it's your work because a poor structure will compromise your success in delivering on your accountability to the board to create and implement strategy. This is not a theoretical matter for you; it's a point of pure self-interest!

The correct structure can release the untapped energies of hundreds and thousands of employees. If employee accountabilities aren't aligned with corporate strategy, they'll work on stuff that is off-strategy. Off-strategy work represents wasted time, effort and opportunity. It carries a significant cost, both emotional and financial. Off-strategy work can also compromise the quality, cost or integrity of on-strategy work.

An additional price is paid when different parts of your company (which are supposed to work together) have different concepts of strategy, and that price is this: your company will disintegrate before your very eyes. So many CEOs and management teams just don't get this. They appear oblivious to their employees and how they are spinning, churning and fighting as they try to get support from peers in another division in order to complete their accountabilities. Some CEOs even *like* their employees to fight it out. They don't understand the angst, misery and lost productivity this causes. They squander employee energy and future shareholder value. They have failed at their jobs through their ignorance of how an organizational structure – thought through, understood and managed by the CEO – can stop this friction and enable the achievement of great results through its employees. This ignorance leads to the creation of company environments that erode the self-worth and confidence of their employees by asking them to do work that is unclearly defined and misaligned to other parts of the organization.

As employees are forced to fill the managerial vacuum, they are often mistrusted and misunderstood by other employees, placing them in unfair and compromising positions to get their work done. They are blamed by their managers for their performance in a structure that sets up no-win situations and failure in performance – a "dark satanic mill," to borrow the words of the poet Milton.

Worse still are the matrix organizations that give employees multiple managers and expect them to balance demands that come at them like bugs hitting a windshield. How can you fairly hold employees accountable for results when two managers are competing for their time and services? As the proverb says, "You cannot serve two masters, for you will love one and hate the other." Or, more likely, hate both.

Some years ago, I coached a senior executive in a major global bank who wanted advice on how to meet the expectations of management. After some discussion, his real challenge to success emerged: he had five bosses to please. When I asked him how he handled them all, his response was very telling: "I hide." This is a sad example of creating organizational dysfunction and setting a person up for failure and poor productivity from the start. This is no way to manage a company. It is exactly what you can avoid if you choose to practice the craft of CEO management.

Structure Drives Behaviour

The structure in which employees find themselves drives most of their behaviour at work. Thus, your choices about the structure of your organization are pivotal to your success. Getting this wrong creates an environment that is negative, undermining and unproductive – an environment that saps the energy, trust and confidence of employees. Getting this right does exactly the opposite: it wins employees' trust, it builds their confidence and it releases their energy and talent.

A clear and organized structure is necessary for a company's work to be done effectively. Good structure increases your organization's capability for handling complexity. It increases its ability to create competitive advantage through innovation and the highly efficient execution and implementation of the enterprise strategy.

You don't believe your organizational structure and roles affect people's behaviours to this degree? See Don't Create a Detention Camp below for an example.

Don't Create a Detention Camp

When you move those difficult, backstabbing so-and-so's into roles that fit them and give them managers who manage them and add value to their work and who take an interest in developing them, they will no longer be such recalcitrant employees. Structure matters. And, as a CEO pointed out to me recently, science bears this out.

In 1971, social psychologist Philip Zimbardo led an experiment to study the impact of structure on people.[24] Zimbardo advertised and hired a group of "normal" young men. He assigned them the role of prisoner or prison guard. Although designed to run two weeks, the study had to be stopped after only six days because the young men – who had been psychologically evaluated as normal – had completely adapted to their roles, and so had Zimbardo and his colleagues.

The guards had become abusive. The prisoners had become dehumanized. The researchers got into their roles as prison managers, worrying about escapes and defiance, not scientific observation.

This and other research shows that the structure people find themselves in changes their behaviour some and how they see the world.

Unfortunately, the organizations that some CEOs lead are similar to that "detention camp," even to the point of enabling unethical behaviour that eventually destroys shareholder value. Good people get caught in these dysfunctional situations and begin to rationalize their unethical behaviours. Trust is absent in relationships between employees, especially between managers and direct reports. Information is withheld. Agreements made in meetings are quickly ignored. Power, politics and subversive sociopathic behaviours on the part of leaders destroy the trust and confidence of employees to get things done. At its worst, this can take down an entire company, as it did in the case of Enron, the Royal Bank of Scotland, Livent Entertainment, Bre-X Minerals and many others. Elliott Jaques called such organizations "paranoiagenic," because when you destroy trust in relationships, you are left with paranoid fear.

But the reverse is also true. When organizations have implemented the principles of the craft of management, they build trust in their relationships. People are transformed by the healthy structure. There is still political jostling and conflict, but it is neutralized by a trust-creating environment.

Be careful that you don't create and run a detention camp as a company. You have a choice.

Choosing the desired functional structure – creating a positive environment for your managers and employees – is your work. I am amazed by the number of CEOs who do not see it this way, who do not see the definition of structure as an important CEO managerial skill that, if mastered, can lead to great success. I often encounter CEOs who fail to see the results they're leaving on the table, CEOs who are pleased with the mediocre performance they get when they could deliver so much more. They need to understand it is good structure that enables the best performance of the company. Bad structure impedes best performance and creates organizational dysfunction.

Bad structure causes the CEO to fail!

First Steps in Creating Your Structure

Your company's structure is the foundation that supports everything it does. To design the structure, you need to disaggregate all of your CEO accountabilities. As the CEO, you know you cannot do it all yourself. That's why you have to break the work into a set of divisions (such as Marketing, Sales, Operations, Logistics, HR, IT, Finance), to which you delegate the accountability and work. The first step of disaggregation is to chunk your accountabilities as CEO into required functions that will report to you, the functions that will enable you to achieve your strategy. This is a chance for you to assess your structure. Too often I see CEOs just accept the status quo. They miss a wonderful opportunity to transform and energize their company.

What Is the Core Function?

The key criterion for choosing the core function – the function around which you can wrap all other functions – is to answer the question, "What drives the revenue?" The answer is the core of your organization, on which everything else hangs. All other functions or divisions exist to enable and maximize the success of this core line process or division. They serve the core function and not their own agendas. List your functions and determine which is at the very core.

For an example of categorizing your accountabilities into functions, consider this list of functions for a retailer:

- Merchandising
- Supply chain
- Real estate
- Marketing
- Sales
- Retail store operations
- Finance
- IT
- Human Resources

Here is a quandary for a retailer and a classic dilemma for the CEO. As illustrated in figure 9, which division is the core? Is it Retail Store Operations, Marketing or Merchandising? How is the work of these divisions to be integrated? Who has the hammer for what? Who is accountable for what? Who will have the authority to tell whom what to do? Leaving these questions unanswered will create untold friction between divisions. The wasted effort and churning will tire and demotivate your employees. Work will feel like being in a 747 with its flaps down: inefficient, ineffective, fatiguing and frustrating.

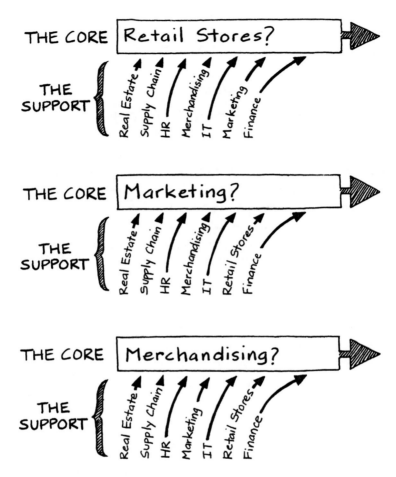

Figure 9: Quandary for a retailer: Which is the core function?

Another way to consider structure is through the metaphor of sculpture. A sculptor cannot build a four-foot-high figure out of clay, because clay does not have the internal support to hold it up; it will collapse. To counter this problem, sculptors invented the armature – twisted wire that is shaped to the intended form, acting like bones to support the clay and the integrity of the whole figure.

The core function of a company is the bone structure that supports and gives it integrity. When you have identified this function, determine what other line functions are required alongside it. You will create a vice-president role for each function, each one reporting to you. Everything hangs off your initial foundational decisions.

In designing the core function, make it as complete as you can. Be careful not to split up the key parts of work so managers and employees have to hand over too many bits of work to other departments. Make it large and whole! For example, one of our clients, a blood collection and testing company, combined into one department all of the work pertaining to collections. Functions that originally were separate – collections, transportation, laboratories and so forth – were combined into one large integrated piece of work. This resulted in significantly reduced interdepartmental handovers. In many respects it simplified managing the business.

This doesn't mean the other divisions are unimportant. Some – especially Marketing and Business Development – may help define and set standards for delivering services required by the customer. However, the importance of non-core functions is in how they *enable* the core function to deliver those services. The external work of a company cannot exist without the internal services provided by the other functions.

You must discuss this task with your senior management team, working with them to make the roles of all other functions very clear: how they support the core. The core function is king. The discussion may be rocky, at first. Clearly identifying the core function may not be popular with executives heading non-core divisions.

I saw this in action when I worked with a mining concern in Eastern Europe to help managers raise productivity. I took them back to basics and audited all of the functions in the structure. Did the role of each function make sense and help achieve the strategy? This required us to meet to hash out the core purpose, which was generally clear to everyone around the table: the extraction and processing of ore. The meeting came to the conclusion that the extraction and processing (E&P) work of the company represented the core. All other functions provided service to them, although they had authority over E&P when it came to things like safety and other regulatory issues.

To my point about initial rockiness: the response of the leaders of the other divisions was fast and furious. They saw no reason to be in service. They protested that they were equal partners in deciding how the mine was run.

We had found the heart of the dysfunction in the organization. After much discussion, the CEO re-clarified the role of each function: E&P were the core, and the rest were service providers. Some of the managers heading the newly designated service divisions refused to make the adjustment and left the company. The productivity of the mine jumped, because clarity about the core drove clarity in other areas. The company had other issues that needed attention, but the core function issue had to be identified and solved first.

Clarifying the functional core of your organization takes time, reflection and dialogue with your team. *But this is your work as CEO.* This is the first of many CEO management decisions you will make, one that will create energy and momentum of purpose for all your employees. The decisions required to implement your conclusions can be awkward and uncomfortable, but avoiding them will create a significant risk to your success and the success of your organization.

Dual Executive Roles

Executives are the functional heads who report to the CEO. The CEO defines what each functional head must accomplish. All functions are accountable to the CEO. Therefore, accountabilities and authority come from the CEO and no one else. Functional heads wear two hats. They are functional managers and members of the executive team; their main role is to deliver on their functional accountabilities. But they also form a collegium of equals, concerned, together, with organizational success without regard to their functional roles.

Nor is this a job once done, done forever. The functional structure must always serve the strategic goals of the company. As Wilfred Brown, CEO of Glacier Metal, observed over fifty years ago:

Effective organization is a function of the work to be done and the resources and techniques available to do it. Thus changes in methods of production bring about changes in the number of work roles, in the distribution of work between roles and in their relationship one to another ... Our observations lead us to accept that optimum organization must be derived from an analysis of the work to be done and the techniques and resources available.[25]

Although the wording may be dated, the meaning is clear: let your structures be guided by the needs of the work necessary to achieve your strategy, not by the whims of the latest management fad. When the strategy changes, the structure must change.

Make Sure You Have All the Wood Behind the Arrowhead

Going back to our example of the company of retail stores, figure 10 shows clear functional alignment should the choice of core function be Retail Store Operations. All of the other divisions (functions) are therefore aligned with the arrowhead, contributing to forward momentum. This is not to say that Retail Store Operations *must* be the core function. For example, if Merchandising or Marketing were chosen as the core function, the divisions of the company would have to be aligned accordingly.

Figure 11 shows a company that is like a splintered arrow, with divisions in misalignment, their work and purpose not in unison and not connected to the core of the organization. This can be the root of much systemic dysfunction in an organization. It takes strong management to get everything connected behind the core function.

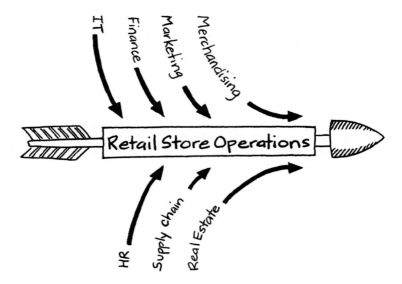

Figure 10: All the wood behind the arrowhead.

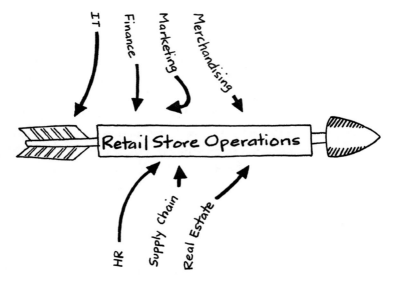

Figure 11: Don't allow the wood to go every which way.

A Solid Foundation

Another way of looking at choosing the desired functional structure is to say that all of your company rests on it the way a house rests on its foundation. Your company's functional structure gives context to all your employees as to where their corporate function fits. This enables you to define clearly how all of the functions of your organization are aligned. The key first step after your strategy is confirmed is to align the bricks of your organization so you can efficiently and effectively begin to implement the strategy.

Which leads us to CEO management principle #3, to be discussed in the following chapter: determining how many levels of work you require in your organization. Allow me one last note, however, before we begin that discussion. Similar to my point made in chapter 3, on the craft of management, just as creating this strategy is not HR's work, but CEO work, so deciding the structure of your company is not their work, but yours. HR may advise you, but how dare you delegate this work! You created the strategy and understand the challenges of implementing it and possess a far-reaching view of where you are taking the company. Given your capability and your management accountability, deciding on the structure is one of the most important decisions to help you implement your strategy. It is your work. HR can give you best advice. And because it is your work, your executive team will regard it as their work, as important management work, as work that all of you should understand and become expert at doing.

Action Steps

Figure 12 gives you a simple diagnostic tool for examining your organization.

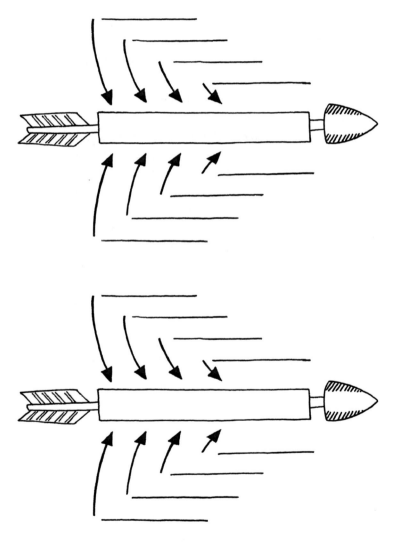

Figure 12: Blank models to determine core and supporting functions.

1. Fill in the template to reflect your organization's structure today.

2. Now fill in the second one, creating your view of your organization's ideal structure.

   a. Is all the wood behind the arrowhead today?
   b. Is your core function identified and clearly known to the entire organization?
   c. Can you create a structure that gives better clarity and focus behind the arrowhead?

You want a structure that energizes your employees, one that minimizes fights among them and enables them to work as effectively and efficiently as possible – the very foundation of competitive advantage.

Executive Summary

1. CEOs generally underestimate or do not understand the power of a clear structure to enable the achievement of their strategy.

2. Your employees' behaviour is driven, more than anything else, by the structure in which they work. Don't construct a detention camp; your employees won't be engaged to the level you require for your organization to be successful.

3. A clear structure enables competitive advantage.

4. Choosing a core function clears things up for your employees.

5. Once you have clarified your core function, lay out with your executive team the functions that support the core function. This is uncomfortable work. But it is *your* work, as CEO.

CHAPTER SIX

CEO Management Principle #3: Level the Organization

Here are the CEO management principles we have discussed so far:

Principle #1:	Create Your Strategy
Principle #2:	Choose Your Organization's Functional Structure

Principle #3, covered in this chapter, is *Level the Organization*. It involves choosing the number of layers required for you to enable your employees to implement your strategy effectively.

How dare you suffocate your organization with too many levels!

Last year I was out to dinner with close friends my wife and I have known for years. In the middle of dinner, one of the guests, Mary, turned to me and asked me about her husband's work situation.

"Nick, you understand how companies work, don't you?" she said. "Can you tell me why James has to suffer the painful experience of working in a company with eleven levels?"

She then proceeded, unprompted by me, to draw and describe the levels on a napkin and describe the pain he was in.

The structure had so many managers checking up on everything that it took ages to get things done; initiative definitely was not rewarded. The work was dull, and there was no clear way forward for people to get promoted. Even if they did get promoted to the next level, it was no big deal, because, in an organization as complex as James's, such promotions represent a micro-step. Furthermore, nobody at the company's lower levels understood the strategy; it was broken into so many small bits of work, level by level, that it wasn't clear how anything contributed to the strategy.

"How can this company survive with a structure like this?" Mary asked.

I was nearly speechless, having just received a concise, relevant and accurate diagnosis of a dysfunctional company. I looked into it afterwards. She was absolutely right. (See figure 13.)

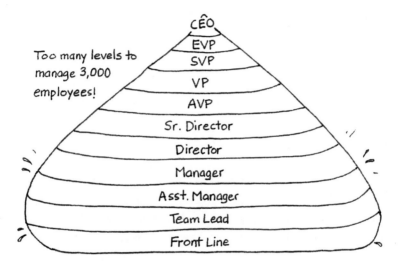

Figure 13: An organization with eleven levels: too many levels to manage 3,000 employees.

Your challenge, as CEO, is to get the levels right in your organization so you can release your employees' energy. Do not suffocate them.

Here's another example, this time a company with 400 employees. (See figure 14.) This company had not eleven but seven levels, but it, too, was choked by too many managers. It didn't help that the company was only ten years old and had entrepreneurial views on managing, weak processes and little discipline to follow them. Employees found themselves in a chaotic environment, totally confused about what was expected of them.

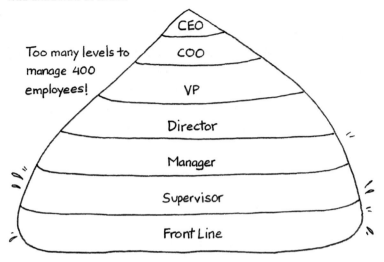

Figure 14: An organization with seven levels – too many levels to manage 400 people.

In both examples, the companies have too many management levels to be truly effective. Managers and employees in such organizations tend to feel suppressed or oppressed by the lack of space or freedom to think for themselves. There is always someone checking up on them. The existence of too many levels compresses work between levels and encourages micromanagement. When a company has too many levels, there is just not enough organizational room at any level to build great roles for employees that generate energy and initiative. Managers in the redundant layers become territorial. They spend their time justifying their existence by creating more and more processes and policies to control what is irrelevant. Too many levels can choke the life out of an organization.

Masters of the craft of management look at bloated companies like doctors. They poke and prod and ask, "What is the right number of levels for this organization?" Too few CEOs examine their organization in this way. Too few ask, "What value do I get from each management layer for the money I pay them?" They appear to just accept the organization's structural status quo. They look elsewhere for cost savings, oblivious to the potential that is created when a company's structure is changed: a significant leap forward in savings, increased employee energy and increased productivity.

Span of Control

Span of control represents the number of roles that report to one manager. There is no rote answer to how many employees can report to one manager. It depends on the level, specialization and diversity of roles reporting to the manager and the complexity of the work. I often encounter the "rule of eight"; I don't endorse its mechanical application unless it checks out with the above criteria – unless it makes sense and can be made to work effectively. That said, I encourage clients to push for broader spans of control, because they make economic sense. However, these spans must not become so broad that they overwhelm and compromise managers' ability to think effectively and add value to the work of their direct reports. Wider spans of control generally mean that managers have more complete, more integrated accountabilities. This is good in itself. Conversely, narrow spans of control lead to smaller, less-integrated jobs that are less fulfilling and cause a greater need for coordination between managers, which is less efficient and less effective.

Title Creep

Much of this over-layering comes from title creep, the process by which unnecessary roles are added to a company. These new roles are almost always prefix roles, those made by simply adding "assistant" or "senior" to a level's title: Assistant Manager, Senior Director or Assistant Vice President. You may have created some of these additional layers yourself when you wanted to keep people happy but had no place to advance them. As you were probably told at some point in your career, "titles are cheap."

Unfortunately, this is not true. Prefix titles can be very costly. They hurt the role of real managers, restricting their autonomy. They reduce the scope and size of a manager's role, decrease the value of the work associated with that role and destroy its capability to add value to the level below it. The manager's original direct reports don't benefit, either. The new assistant role compromises employee independence to make decisions and takes interesting work from them. Ultimately, vitality is leeched out of the organization.

Often managers create new prefix roles because of their inability to deal with the performance issue of the person just above the new role. "We need to shore him up with an assistant," a senior manager may say. However, these managers don't need shoring up; they need replacing! They are unable to do their work because they lack the capability to do it. Anytime you place capable people under a manager who cannot add value, you hurt your employees. We are back to creating detention camps again.

Too many levels in an organization are the curse of effectiveness and efficiency. Organizations become obese when CEOs don't understand the drag these extra layers put on productivity and profitability.

How dare you let an escalation of titles happen on your watch!

On the other side of this issue, you will encounter challenges when you do need to add a level. For example, your company may be facing significant change. Though you have determined the number of levels for your organization, you may conclude that you require an additional level to handle the added complexity and uncertainty caused by the change. This new role and level may be required for two years. Once the assignment is complete, the role and level can be discontinued. When adding levels to your organization, be clear about the cost (it can be in the millions of dollars), the results you will get from this investment and the "best by" date: the point at which the role will be considered redundant and removed.

Resistance to Rationalizing Roles

Be aware that your managers will resist your decision to rationalize titles into fewer titles, even more than they will resist pay grade changes. They will argue that replacing their title of "Associate Vice President" with "Director" will be seen in the marketplace as a demotion. They will argue that their recruitment of new people to their team will be hurt by their more lowly title.

It's true that some employees are "title status conscious." Our clients find that this issue decreases in intensity, however, as employees are given great work to do and realize that their new role *does* have status: the role they have been given is large and challenging, with complex work and full discretion to make decisions. They realize that they are in a role in which they will learn new skills; a role in which they can create value and have an impact; a role, in fact, that leads to greater accountability and career advancement in the longer term.

One of our clients told me about a manager in charge of credit processing for external banking clients who came to his CEO with a request for a title change.

"When I attend meetings at our bank with outside people, there are twenty of us in the room, and I am the only manager," this person said. "Everyone else is a VP or a senior director. Is it possible you could give me a more appropriate title, say, director or vice president?"

The CEO thought for a few moments and replied, "I'm not going to do that now, but let's meet in six months. If you still feel strongly about this then, I'll give it some serious thought. Right now, no go."

Six months later, they met again.

"So, what do you think?" the CEO asked.

"Well, actually, I am very proud of my title," the manager said. "I can see in those meetings, now, that I have a bigger role and more authority than anyone else attending. The scope of my work and the trust placed in me to do it have made my request unnecessary."

And that is the key. Keeping the levels in an organization to a minimum allows you to create large, meaty jobs with significant accountability and authority, jobs that make your employees proud of their title and the work they do.

Problems Associated with Too Many Levels

Title creep may be a core causal problem, but it's not the only problem suffered by companies that are fat and non-optimally layered. Let's see just where fattening the organization can lead.

Communication

Did you ever play the old party game when you were a child called Broken Telephone, or Rumour? You know, the one where everybody sat in a circle, somebody created a message and whispered it to the person seated beside them, and on it went until the last child repeated the message for the whole group – a message that, by then, was totally different.

Now look at the eleven-level and seven-level company examples in figures 13 and 14 (pages 75 and 76), in which there is too big a gap between the CEO and the front line. Multiple levels make it harder for a CEO to communicate effectively down through the organization. Over time, he or she will be in danger of becoming some mythical figure who is irrelevant to the day-in and day-out realities of getting front-line work done. Likewise, with this many levels, feedback from the front line will not get to the top with anything like the meaning the sender intended.

Some companies create communications departments to combat this. This is well-intentioned but can let managers off the hook of their accountability to set context for their employees. Managers should be able to tell employees everything they need to know about the company and the work they expect them to do. Managers certainly should not hear, at the same time as their employees, about significant strategic initiatives or other news from the communications department.

Roles Are Too Close and Confining

A structure with too many levels also makes roles feel confining. There's not enough room to do real work or make real decisions.

Over-layering constrains employees' freedom to act. They spend too much time bumping up against others in roles too close to theirs. Few distinctions between management levels exist. Employees disengage and simply show up to collect their pay. They'd like to do great work, but they have learned from hard experience that it's not possible – that it actually appears to be unwanted.

Managers Don't Add Value

Managers in a fat organization often don't have enough distance between them and the work of their direct reports to add any real value. They end up doing little more than scheduling vacations, creating bureaucratic budgets and providing ineffective performance reviews. Accountability becomes confused or is thrown out altogether. As for those under the manager, they become bored, because they lack the space to create and do meaty chunks of real work. The manager's direct reports begin to share their work with their manager, who welcomes the opportunity to micromanage, because there's no higher-level work for them to do to add value.

Working like this isn't challenging and, in the end, isn't satisfying. The company survives, but only because employees feel responsible enough to keep things moving. However, work that is driven by responsibility alone can compromise and even undermine a CEO's enterprise strategy.

Span of Control Is Too Narrow

Managers who cannot add value to employees' work are often given fewer direct reports, which narrows their span of control. (See also page 77.) The result invites micromanagement. A manager wants to justify being a manager. There is no employee unluckier than one who is a manager's single direct report. Talk about undivided attention! The employee becomes the centre of their manager's universe.

Span of control should be designed to *disable* a manager from micromanaging. Make the span broad enough that the manager can control the scope and context of direct reports and have time to monitor and coach as required – but not interfere. Managers hire employees to do their work. They must let them do it.

Money Is Wasted

Extra management layers cost money, not only in the personnel costs of salary, unemployment, insurance and taxes but also in lost productivity. I see this constantly as I help companies reorganize more productively. When they lose layers, they gain productivity. Extra layers keep good work from being done. Adding insult to injury, the best employees leave, looking for challenging and satisfying work – often enriching a competitor's human capital.

Too Many Meetings, Too Few Decisions

More levels = more people = more meetings. Meetings are crowded because the only way to make a decision is through consensus. No one has been given the authority to make the decision, or the authority they've been given is unclear. Nor is it clear who (if anyone) is accountable for the results of the decision, or who holds whom accountable.

Can decisions even get made in such organizations? Obviously they can, because we all know organizations that fit this description. But the decisions come only after the slow bureaucratic slog of endless meetings with seemingly everyone present to ensure that everyone is onside.

Fattened or Flattened?

Too many layers make an organization fat and clumsy, but is there also a danger that, in aiming for leanness, we might end up all skin and bones? The famous knowledge expert Ikujiro Nonaka showed that middle managers serve a vital role in an enterprise's creation and storage of knowledge. In an article in the *Ivey Business Journal*, Paul Osterman of the MIT Sloan School of Management has shown the importance of middle managers in implementing strategic decisions.[26] We know we should be leaner but don't want to become too lean. Finding the optimal number of management layers is a true executive managerial skill, task and accountability.

You don't have to have a fat company. Nor do you have to be all skin and bones. An optimally levelled company is lean without being emaciated – it is fit, not anorexic. The goal is to create a structure in which each layer of management adds value to the layers below.

How Many Levels Do You Need to Implement Your Strategy? Differentiate them!

Optimizing your management levels is part of your work as a master of the craft of executive management. Like the rest of the craft, it is something you have not been trained to do.

Implementing your strategy requires different thinking at different levels of your organization. Different thinking means different work. Your work as CEO is different from the work of your vice presidents. Their work is different from the work of their directors. The directors' work is different from their managers. The critical issue for you is to differentiate the work of the levels of your organization. If you do this effectively, you will be able to clarify the number of levels required for you to implement your strategy. Mary's story, at the beginning of this chapter, of an eleven-level organization is an example of poor differentiation.

The Hierarchy of Capability

To summarize, to master the structure of your organization, you must identify the types of work in your organization, differentiate it and organize it. And never forget: all of this work is in the service of your strategy. Figure 15 categorizes the overall work of your organization into three layers, each of which contains various levels.

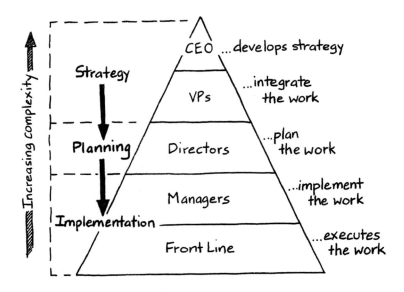

Figure 15: The hierarchy of capability.

1. *Strategy*: The top and smallest layer is a team of employees who can create the enterprise strategy – you and your vice presidents. They must be capable of synthesizing the more intangible, abstract strategic challenges that face the organization into a coherent and winning strategic plan. Their role is to align and integrate the work of the organization and start the process of translating strategy into an understandable, engaging conversation with the next layer.

2. *Planning*: The middle layer of the organization translates the abstract strategy into tangible plans that build the systems and processes necessary to effectively implement it. These roles – directors – are critical to the success of your organization.

3. *Implementation*: The bottom layers, made up of managers and front-line employees, implement the middle layer's (directors') plans, getting the work done and delivering the annual plan. This is the layer that engages and delivers value to the customer. It is the layer where most employees work. To implement effectively,

employees require well-planned work systems, processes and technology to enable and ease the burden of their work, and managers who add value to their work and are seen to help them, not hinder them.

Front-line employees require the greatest clarity in their work; they benefit significantly from effective operational planning above them. This is also the group that suffers the most when management does not manage effectively. Bad management limits their choices and decision-making, because they have the least power, discretion and judgment. Their managers must not shirk their executive work; they must set these employees up for success.

This pragmatic model is designed to help you review the critical work that you require to be done and determine which organizational layer should do it to ensure its successful completion. If you place this work too low in your organization, where employees do not have the capability to do the work effectively, you will be disappointed with the results.

Greater Complexity Requires Organizational Skills

From the first day you started to manage, you have faced complexity, because managerial work means using your discretion and judgment to solve delegated tasks of complexity. From that day on, the higher you rose in the management structure, the more complex the problems you were given to solve. The more complex your problems, the more important organizing the work of others became.

Now you run an entire organization. The structure you build becomes a critical tool that enables you to successfully accomplish your strategy and solve the complex challenges you face. As you manage more and more people, organizing their work becomes critical to the success of the company.

Find Your Company's Optimal Number of Layers

Let's look at the number of levels you need, using a freestanding business unit (BU) as a point of reference.

A business unit is an organization that has complete control over its profit & loss (P&L) and contains all of the business functions required for autonomous action. It actually can be carved out of the organization and sold as a free-standing unit.

In general, I would expect a business unit to have five levels, from CEO to front-line employees. (See figure 16.)

A business unit might have four levels when:

1. It is really too small (say 250 employees or less) to support a greater investment in management, or

2. There is little need for the CEO to develop strategy.

A business unit might have six levels when it is exceptionally large (i.e., greater than 3,000 employees) and works with highly complex processes. An example of this would be a retail division of a large bank.

In other words, stick with five levels as the normative case for a business unit and discuss four- and six-level BUs as occasional but justifiable departures from the norm.

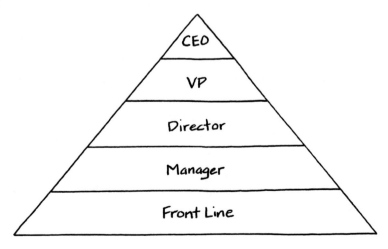

Figure 16: Example of a five-level organization.

A six-level organization (see figure 17) consists of a portfolio of business units with some corporate support groups at the centre. Such a portfolio needs to be reasonably coherent, with organizing/ selection criteria based on common principles that give the BUs a common thread of purpose (e.g., different operating companies in the same related industries).

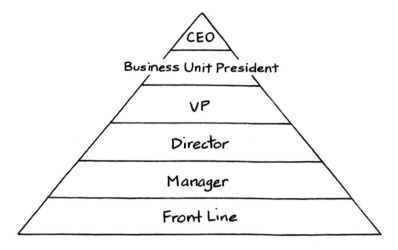

Figure 17: Example of a six-level organization.

A seven-level organization (see figure 18) consists of a number of groups, each of which is a portfolio of coherently selected business units making for an employee population of about 2,000 employees. Each group is a separate six-level organization. Each BU will have some corporate support functions (such as Finance, Human Resources and IT) that report to the level-seven CEO, and probably some group support functions that report to the level-six vice president or whatever the role is called. In general, an organization with seven levels can have 25,000+ employees.

Regardless of the number of levels, if you are the CEO of an entire organization with clear accountability for the P&L, you are the only person with complete accountability and authority for the working environment within which each and every employee does their best work. This is true whether you have 250, 1,000, 5,000, 10,000, 50,000 or 120,000+ employees in your organization. There are few organizations that need eight levels; these would be large multi-national companies such as General Electric (GE).

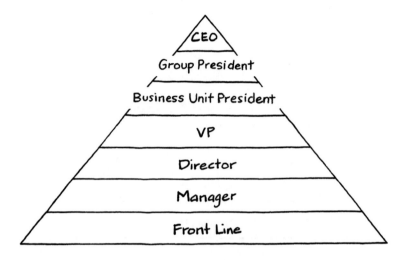

Figure 18: Example of a seven-level organization.

Design Can Be Top-Down or Bottom-Up

In determining the number of levels for the organization, you have the choice of designing it top-down or bottom-up. I use both processes equally in my consulting work with clients. Some clients naturally start at the top; some naturally start at the bottom. Occasionally clients start at the top, work down through the entire organization; then, having reached the bottom level, they check it by working back up to the top again. The choice is yours.

Top-Down Design

Step 1: To determine the levels, continue to disaggregate your work. (See figure 19.) In CEO management principle #2, we showed you how to disaggregate the CEO's accountabilities into functional buckets, driven by strategy. You identified the core function and determined the other functions that were required alongside it.

Step 2: Organize the support functions (e.g., Finance, HR, IT) into VP groupings based on their strategic significance and size. The key question for you is, "Which support function heads must I have sitting at my executive table?"

Now that you have chosen your executive team, you need to take two more steps:

Step 3: Disaggregate each function into director groups organized by a coherent set of processes, products or services.

Step 4: Disaggregate the director groups into management groups tightly organized by the work done at the front line.

STEP 1: CEO confirms strategy, confirms functions

STEP 2: CEO disaggregates strategy to the functions

STEP 3: Functional VPs disaggregate work to groups of Directors

STEP 4: Directors disaggregate work to Managers

Managers closely knit to Front Line

Figure 19: Top-down design.

Bottom-Up Design

To determine the levels from the bottom up, start with the front line. Give each value-adding management level above the front line a single title to describe the management it does. Add layers to the top but keep the bottom three layers constant.

Doing this during growth gives your front-line employees an environment with maximum clarity and consistency. All employees require clarity, but none more than the front line. They have the least autonomy and decision-making authority to change things. They have the narrowest view of your strategy. You must protect them and enhance their ability to get things done. Let the burden of reorganizations be borne by levels with more leeway.

Figure 20 shows how an organization can grow, by adding a layer to the top when you go to a new level of complexity or to the side for handling larger quantities of the same type. The front-line, manager and director levels remain intact. Any additional levels are added above them.

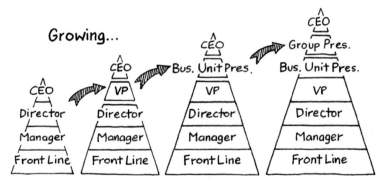

Figure 20: How an organization can grow.

If the company downsizes (see figure 21), the bottom three levels will remain constant, and the integrity of the structure should stand. The essential work done at each of the levels will remain the same. The number of employees doing the work would need to be reduced. However, if the downsizing demands the removal of levels of work, the first level to be removed is the top one – yours. For a seven-level organization, the CEO becomes a level-six CEO, or if it is decided that two levels have to be removed, the CEO becomes a level-five CEO. This enables the organization to reduce levels efficiently and effectively.

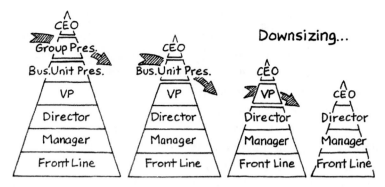

Figure 21: How an organization can downsize.

Following are the six steps of bottom-up design.

Step 1: Start with the core function. Identify the capabilities you want in front-line teams and give each team a front-line manager.

Step 2: Assemble front-line managers into groups connected by a common process or set of services.

Step 3: Aggregate these teams into functions and give each one a functional VP.

Step 4: Do the same thing for other line functions and again for support functions.

Step 5: Test the result against your rules for span of control.

Step 6: Review and repeat cycle as necessary.

Getting the right number of levels for your organization can be challenging. Others can consult to you, assist you and help you implement your decisions, but you are accountable for the final decisions. As the CEO, this is your work.

Examine the different levels of work you require to implement your strategy. What type of thinking and work do you require? As discussed on pages 83–85 and shown in figure 15, I suggest that the bottom three levels represent the required operational planning and implementation levels to make things happen. Beware of title creep! Each level should have one title for the work done at the level. In this instance, I suggest director and manager. Avoid prefixes, which will muddy the waters and reduce the size and meatiness of the work. No Senior Directors and no Assistant Managers.

Next, decide how many additional levels you require above levels 1, 2 and 3. What is the complexity of the thinking and strategic planning work? Look again at figure 15. Do you require five levels? Now look back at the examples in figures 17 and 18. Always try, at the beginning of this exercise, to limit the number of levels. Be aware of what a level of management can cost you and what you will get in return, in terms of value. In my experience, when CEOs perform this audit, they can find a level of management expertise that costs them millions of dollars but adds questionable value. Be biased towards fewer, rather than more, levels. It is much easier to add a level later than to eliminate one.

At this point you have determined the optimal number of management layers for your organization. Usually this means you have to consolidate some roles. You can start this off by getting rid of the prefix-manager roles and entirely eliminating others. This raises an important question: What work needs to be done in the roles of these new levels? You must next align the work done in the roles to the corporate strategy and integrate the roles so they are headed in a single direction. You do this with the people who report directly to you, your senior leadership team. The next chapter discusses how to define the work.

Action Steps

1. Take a moment to consider the existing levels in your organization. First, start at the CEO's office and go down, counting each layer of management in the reporting structure. Then start at the bottom and go up. Next, try it again, starting with a different department. Repeat it with yet another one. Now answer the following questions:

- How many layers does it take from the lowest-level worker to get to you, the CEO?
- Did you count all of the prefix-titles as levels? They are!
- Did you find differences in levels between one function and another?
- What value does each title at each level of management add?
- How much does each level of your organization cost in salaries?
- Do you get the required value for the money you spend for each level?
- Is there a level of management that suffocates the level below it?
- What are the potential savings should a level be removed?

2. If you could start with a clean slate and with endless initial resources, how would you structure the layers in your company to best deliver on your strategy?

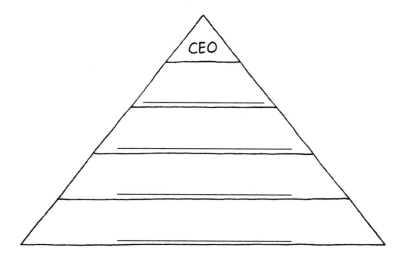

Figure 22: Fill in your level titles.

Executive Summary

1. No matter what size your organization is, it probably has too many levels.

2. Having too many levels in an organization reduces the scope and size of work assignments in your organization, allows mismanagement and suffocates the individual spirit, energy and innovative opportunities of employees.

3. Title creep will turn your organization into a de-energized, costly, unproductive bureaucracy.

4. Create an organization with fewer levels, broad spans of control and large, juicy, challenging roles for your employees. The work will energize them.

CHAPTER SEVEN

CEO Management Principle #4: Define the Work

Let's recap the principles covered so far.

Principle #1:	Create Your Strategy
Principle #2:	Choose Your Organization's Functional Structure
Principle #3:	Level the Organization

Now we come to principle #4: *Define the Work*.

One of our clients runs video clips on a television in their reception lobby highlighting the progress of initiatives, accomplishments, messages from the CEO and employee profile interviews.

One day the president was walking through the lobby and stopped to watch an interview with a recently hired manager. The manager was comparing his new job with his past job experience. To the president's dismay, the manager proclaimed loudly and energetically: "It's great here. I can do anything I want. I have total freedom!"

How dare you leave your employees guessing at their work!

Obviously, no one had set the context and accountability for this manager in terms of implementing the company's strategy. The president liked the idea of his employees feeling empowered, but to what end? An organization's projects and strategies need to be implemented to a set of specific measurements. No wonder the implementation of his strategy was falling behind. He needed to recalibrate his senior management team using the CEO management principles.

Figure 23: Fake empowerment.

Laissez-Faire Empowerment

Do you remember the empowerment fad that swept across North America in the 1990s? Managers appeared to have an epiphany.

"We're not getting enough creativity, innovation or energy from our employees," they said. "The answer is to empower them! Get rid of all the restrictions ... be empowered ... go for it!"

Some employees took their managers at their word and seized the day, only to get pulled back or slapped down. Often the empowerment directive was given without context or limits. But limits clearly existed in managers' minds, and employees were quickly schooled in their importance. (See Figure 23.)

Other employees looked in vain for boundaries within which to do their freshly empowered work. Their experience with obscure boundaries taught them to distrust management's intentions with "the empowerment thing." They held back to avoid grasping what they rightly perceived was a prickly nettle.

Soon enough the whole initiative was revealed for the ill-conceived fad that it was. It failed because it allowed managers to be even less clear and direct about the work that they wanted done.

What Employees Want to Know

Employees who are truly empowered are clear about the work they are expected to do. They know what outputs are intended and the boundaries within which they must accomplish them. They know who has what authority and who holds what accountability. That clarity is supposed to come from their manager. It is the foundation of fairness in every manager–direct report relationship.

Here's what employees tell us they need in order to feel and be empowered:

- Good context so they can see how their job fits into a larger whole
- Clear accountabilities, with clear definitions of success
- The authorities they need to deliver on their accountabilities
- The resources, tools and processes they need to do the work properly
- Adequate training so they have the skills they need
- Fair pay
- A clear description of their cross-functional lateral relationships (see more on this in the next chapter)
- Clearly stated guardrails: the boundaries they cannot cross, which may be policies or performance constraints (e.g., keep service levels at 98% and costs no higher than $20 per call)

Ensuring that employees get these things is a fundamental accountability of executive management. In the previous two chapters, I showed you how to gain a clear picture of your organization's structure – its functions and levels. This chapter concentrates on the roles inside these – on defining the accountabilities and outputs you expect from each employee.

Children need sandboxes that are big enough to play in and have fun, but not so big that they feel lost and overwhelmed. So it is with employees. One size does not fit all. Each role requires an employee who fits it. In a good person–job fit, the role feels like a sandbox with edges that can just be touched with outstretched fingertips. Role boundaries are defined and generous enough to stretch the employee beyond his or her comfort zone, but not so big as to feel threatening. (See figure 24.) Within this right-fitting role, the employee should be able to get the work done as he or she sees fit, as long as these actions are within the company's policies.

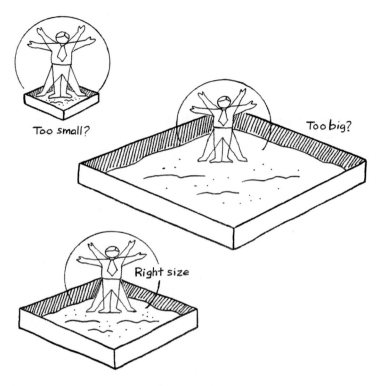

Figure 24: Create the right-sized sandbox.

Your task, then, is to define the work of the role of each employee, to help you and them achieve the enterprise strategy and create organizational momentum. Employees do their best work when they know what is expected and how it ties back into the strategy cascade. Getting this right empowers them. Getting it wrong disempowers them. It breeds uncertainty and insecurity; it stifles innovation and compromises performance.

Defining roles is a process of dialogue by which your organization constantly refines and optimizes work processes. This dialogue enables employees who encounter gray areas of accountability or duplicated work to approach their manager for clarification. Ongoing adjustments to roles (and authorities – see the next chapter, on principle #5) are a fact of life. Because no plan survives intact at the initial implementation stage, this work requires ongoing conversations between managers and employees.

Competitive Advantage

Clarity about the work that you manage, built on the foundation of structure and levels, enables you to create a competitive advantage. Your job is to align all of the work (every role) of your employees and keep it focused on implementing the organization's strategy. Many CEOs don't understand the sheer tenacity and persistence required for this process to succeed. Their abdication of this CEO management work stalls the accomplishment of their strategy.

When you don't define the work, your employees fill the vacuum. They find some other way to resolve the uncertainty, and this invariably undermines the enterprise strategy. Why would you ever think that your strategy will be implemented by employees who are forced to *guess* what they should be doing?

Those of your employees who thrive on ambiguity will love this situation. They relish not being managed closely. They love having the freedom to do what they want to do and not what they should do. Ironically, organizations often reward such employees in annual performance reviews for their success in doing work that actually *undermines* the enterprise strategy.

Most employees, if uncertain about their work, will stall to varying degrees, depending on their confidence, as they try to define the work they think they should do. They will spend an inordinate amount of time trying to get services and support from peers in other divisions, peers who are equally unclear and unsure of what *they* should be doing and what authority *they* have in providing that service.

Failing to define the work raises other issues as well:

- Attempts to build a fair, transparent compensation system fail because there is no clear, up-to-date definition of work to be valued in each role
- Recruiting talent is hit-or-miss because no one can accurately describe the work of the role for which the company is recruiting

- Coaching and monitoring employee performance issues misfires; no one knows what the work or performance metrics are, so they cannot judge whether jobs are being done well
- Talent development processes cannot be effectively managed, because no one can clearly describe future career paths
- Meetings bog down as decision-making devolves into consensus because no one has the accountability and authority for decisions; the effectiveness of the decision-making process collapses across the organization
- Committees are actually formed because employees are afraid of making a decision
- You as CEO and your functional heads cannot grant discretion or authority because you have to actually know what the work is first

Unfortunately, the above points describe what organizational life looks like to so many of us. We start thinking that things should be better but quickly become fatigued at the prospect of change, given how hard we already have to fight to be effective managers in the current environment.

Managers Cannot Delegate This – It Is *Their* Work

I come across many managers who ask their employees to write their own role descriptions and define their own work. But surely this is the ultimate act of managerial abdication! It may be okay to ask employees to propose, or draft or provide input, but defining the roles and accountabilities of direct reports is your job, because it is fundamental to the craft of management.

Managers hire direct reports to do work for them in order to accomplish large pieces of work. The role of managers is not to ask their employees what their work is. It is to define the roles of their direct reports – including the accountabilities – and then to align and integrate their work in the organization. What is a manager's value-add if they duck this work? By definition, a manager is someone who is accountable for the work of other people. It's suicidal for a manager not to define that work.

Presumably, these managers were hired for their skills and capability. To be respected by their direct reports, they need to be seen as more capable than those they manage. Employees' managers should have a broader purview of the organization and a deeper understanding of the corporate strategy. This is what enables them to scope and allocate work more effectively than their direct reports. Doing this work requires innovation and integration of strategic issues and solutions to meet and overcome impending strategic challenges.

For example, one of our clients tells the following story.

"We had sixty to seventy employees in our collections call centre, and most of them wanted to be transferred out of there to another department in the company. They liked the company, but not collections. This was a challenge, as collections are an essential piece of our work.

"I asked HR why employees were dissatisfied. The answer I got was that they were really stressed in not being able to talk to the customer enough. So we did an hourly breakdown on what work was done and found out that employees, on average, actually talked only eighteen minutes per hour to customers. They spent the rest of the time dialling, making notes into the system and doing other administrative duties. Forty-two minutes of each hour was spent in non-value-added stuff – dull, mechanical work.

"To counter this, we brought in the latest collection system software that featured automatic dialling, with customer files that popped up on the screen so they no longer had to search for hard copy files. We also gave employees more discretion on payment plans with the customers.

"After we had implemented these changes, I received a call from the company in California that ran our biannual employee survey. They asked me, 'What are you doing? We have never seen morale numbers in a collection division so high anywhere else in North America!' Employees were now talking to customers forty-eight minutes per hour, and we were able to help customers who had temporary financial difficulties. That's why it was so much fun to figure it out and to get those results."

How to Define Roles

Defining the work of the organization starts at the top: you must define your own role as CEO, with direction and input from your board. This is the one exception to the rule that employees do not define their own roles. And you must define your own accountabilities, too.

I suggest you use the format of the role definition form shown in figure 25. I am not big on job descriptions. They require too much detail and tend to be a list of activities. As a result, they become quickly outdated.

A role definition form has two key points. First, it asks you to answer the question, "If I do my role right, what outputs will I accomplish?" This helps you think in terms of results, not activities. It's the results that matter to you. In the space provided you should be able to synthesize your list of outputs into a maximum of two sentences.

After you have done this, determine the five or six accountabilities that are required to accomplish what you have described as the output of the CEO role. Limit it to six – this will force you to focus and achieve clarity in your thinking. Annual goals, the authorities required for the role and executive behaviours are added later, making this a useful management document that is concise and clear about your expectations of your direct reports.

Your role as CEO will be described in reasonably abstract words. For example, in the case of the CEO in figure 25: "If I do my job right ... the organization will be positioned as the national leader in our market in Canada by 2020. It will have been transformed in every aspect of its business to enable it to secure cumulative, increased performance and predictable value for our shareholders."

The meaning implicit in the words "national leader in our market in Canada" has significant implications and will have to be unpacked into a series of strategies. It is very clear, however, that this CEO will have to build the company into a national leader by 2020. This is great context for all employees.

Role Definition Form

Role Title:	CEO
Incumbent:	Pat Singh

Purpose of Role: If I Do My Job Right, I Will Accomplish the Following Outputs:

The organization will be positioned as the national leader in our market in Canada by 2020. It will have been transformed in every aspect of its business to enable it to secure cumulative, increased performance and predictable value for our shareholders.

I am accountable to:

1. Create corporate strategy to achieve the business goals of the company and satisfy the key shareholders of the company for the next five to ten years.
2. Build the talent and capability of the employees of the company to a level that creates competitive advantage in our industry.
3. Ensure that Operations performs at a level in which the quality and assurance of performance makes the company the market leader in our industry.
4. Consolidate the support areas of the business and optimize the divisions' capability to support the core business – Operations.
5. Establish key performance indicators required to determine organizational progress and enable all managers to manage effectively against the business plan.

Figure 25: Example, role definition of CEO, level 5.

Completing your own role definition will help you see the work you want your direct reports to do. Your next job is to create role definitions for each of them and then meet with them, one-on-one, to ensure that they understand what the role is and the work that you will hold them accountable to successfully complete. Then your direct reports will go through the same process with their own direct reports. The process continues through each management level down to the front line.

I call this the accountability cascade. Another way to look at it is to refer to it as a strategy cascade, for if the work has been defined correctly, it will be completely aligned to your strategy.

A Note on Defining the Work of Your Senior Management Team

When you determined your organization's functional structure, you chose the functions or divisions that must report to your role to achieve the enterprise's strategic goals. An executive manager role heads each of these functions and these managers must do the type of work required at this level. For example, a five-level organization (as defined in the previous chapter) would require functional heads to do the work that we defined as at the vice-president level. Each of these positions will have to be defined by you; you must clearly specify the roles, expected outcomes and key accountabilities.

An executive role definition is much like executive work itself: it is abstract and high-level. Resist the urge to over-detail work that is by definition strategic. Insist that executive roles do not include descriptions of the operational work that should be described as part of their direct reports' roles.

Executives can find the abstract, strategic nature of the work unsettling as they manage ever-increasing levels of complexity and uncertainty. As their discomfort increases, some will seek refuge by doing the operational work of their director-level direct reports. Executive role definitions must focus on outcomes that are high-level and on managing lower-level managers with an eye to *their* accountability for operational excellence.

Role Definition Examples

Over the next few pages, you will find examples of the role definitions of a five-level company. In each case, the different management levels have different types of work, cascading down from the vice-president level to the director, manager and front-line levels. (For your reference, figure 26 shows the structure of a five-level company.)

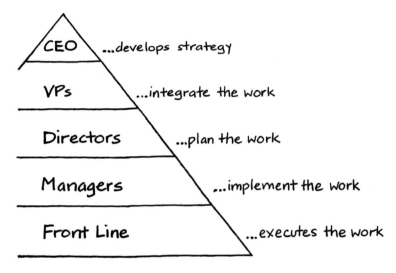

Figure 26: A five-level organization and its work at each level.

The examples that follow may look simple, but the way they force differentiation of the work between levels releases the power of the organization. This process will cause a great deal of discussion, because what could be more relevant to each of your direct reports than their roles? When you get down to the nitty-gritty of each role, employees pay attention. It is paramount to them to understand and agree to the work for which they are going to be held accountable. Think of the competitive advantage you can create if you can clarify this in every manager–direct report relationship in your organization.

Role Definition Form	
Role Title:	Vice President, Operations
Incumbent:	Clive Nation
Manager's Role:	CEO
Manager's Name:	Pat Singh

Purpose of Role: If I Do My Job Right, I Will Accomplish the Following Outputs:

The organization will have a scalable, efficient operational capability that is designed to meet strategic requirements and deliver high-value service over the next two to five years.

Accountabilities

1. Translate corporate strategy into a cohesive, national Operations strategy while creating synergies wherever possible, over the next two to five years.
2. Determine the method and pace of change needed to move the current operation to strategy.
3. Develop the integrated Operations Plan. Harmonize the overall integration of work while taking into consideration contingencies for ensuring appropriate scalability.
4. Manage operational performance to specified quality standards.
5. Manage operational risk. Identify and mitigate potential risks that could impede the implementation of our strategy.
6. Build the talent and capability of the employees in division to a level that creates competitive advantage in our industry.

Figure 27: Example, role definition of vice president, level 4.

Role Definition Form	
Role Title:	Director, Operations – Manitoba
Incumbent:	LaShaun Cook
Manager's Role:	Vice President, Operations
Manager's Name:	Clive Nation

Purpose of Role: If I Do My Job Right, I Will Accomplish the Following Outputs:
Build and manage the Operations systems and plans in Manitoba capable of efficiently and effectively meeting our delivery standards and strategic goals.

Accountabilities
1. Build a one- to two-year Operations plan for the region. Create the processes and systems to maximize efficiency and effectiveness of Operations in Manitoba.
2. Plan, execute and monitor performance of Operations to ensure that performance meets our delivery standards and commitments to the customer.
3. Develop and maintain Business Recovery Plans to ensure sustainability of Operations.
4. Assess, measure and benchmark performance to internal and external best practice, continually challenging the status quo to improve performance and sustainability of Operations in Manitoba.
5. Ensure that Operations' organizational structure and employee capability meet present and future needs. Develop talent and maintain succession-planning processes to ensure that we have the talent to sustain and grow Operations.
6. Build the talent and capability of the employees in our region to a level that creates competitive advantage.

Figure 28: Example, role definition of director, level 3.

Role Definition Form	
Role Title:	Manager, Analytical Services, Operations
Incumbent:	Grania Cookson
Manager's Role:	Director, Operations – Manitoba
Manager's Name:	LaShaun Cook

Purpose of Role: If I Do My Job Right, I will Accomplish the Following Outputs:

Manage high-quality continuous improvement processes in Operations to effectively and efficiently meet our delivery standards and operational goals.

Accountabilities

1. Build an annual business plan for Analytical Services.
2. Monitor and analyse performance of processes to ensure that outcomes meet our delivery standard and operational goals.
3. Anticipate problems, identify root cause, develop methodologies and implement mitigation processes that prevent reoccurrence of an issue.
4. Plan and schedule work to achieve optimum productivity and efficient workflow in a risk-free environment.
5. Leverage knowledge and best practices to optimize team performance to meet goals. Apply value-stream thinking.
6. Ensure that employee capability meets present and future needs. Develop talent and maintain succession-planning processes to ensure that we have employees to sustain and grow Operations.

Figure 29: Example, role definition of manager, level 2.

Role Definition Form	
Role Title:	Team Lead, Operations
Incumbent:	Dan Leasing
Manager's Role:	Manager, Analytical Services, Operations – Manitoba
Manager's Name:	Grania Cookson

Purpose of Role: If I Do My Job Right, I Will Accomplish the Following Outputs:

Execute tasks as directed by the manager, ensuring efficient workflow and quality processes to meet our delivery standards and operational goals on a weekly basis.

Accountabilities

1. Ensure scheduling of personnel to achieve optimum productivity and efficient workflow, as directed by their manager.
2. Assign routine tasks to team members as directed by their manager. Provide an appraisal of the effectiveness of the task.
3. Ensure compliance with processes.
4. Provide recommendations to the manager on employee performance, financial variance and requirements for current and new technologies.
5. Assign tasks, as directed by their manager, in compliance with quality management systems to meet accreditation requirements.

Figure 30: Example, role definition of team lead, level 1.

Delegate Using QQTRs to Create Clarity and Fairness

When you assign a role, you assign accountabilities with tasks. You need to specify the results you want for each task: the Quantity, Quality, Time and Resources (QQTRs). Setting QQTRs is part of management planning work. Many managers have a tough time communicating the exact specifications for task completion to a direct report because they have no model like QQTR to use as a reference. I certainly have found, through experience, that these four criteria are excellent for clarifying expectations with employees.

Quantity: How much of something needs to be produced? Generally, this is easy to specify.

Quality: What is the standard that will be applied to determine if something is "good enough"? Quality is a more difficult measurement to determine, because often it is subjective. It takes time for both managers and direct reports to understand what acceptable quality looks like and how it is to be judged as acceptable. The process of trial and error helps determine this.

Time: By when does this activity need to be produced? Generally, this is easy to specify.

Resources: What resources does the direct report require to complete the task? This can be difficult to clarify. The category "resources" is there to call out managers who have few resources to give and cope by trying to delegate tasks to their direct reports without assigning the required resources. This is blatantly unfair to employees. This is where employees' best advice and dialogue really count. A dialogue about resources should be trust enhancing.

The whole purpose of QQTRs is to create clarity and openness around work that employees are held accountable to complete effectively.

When setting QQTRs, you always have to specify which one of the four criteria can be flexible. As the manager, you have to make a choice: On what are you willing to compromise? Quality? Quantity? Time? Resources? There's a reason for doing this: if you do not clearly specify which element is flexible, employees will always compromise on Quality. People fail to deliver projects to your expectations when they don't realize what is really important to you. When setting QQTRs, you must focus employees on what is important.

For example, let's look at the systems implementation of a new accounting system. The project has to be fully implemented using 50% custom code (not more) to specs, has to be done by x Time, and Resources are not tightly restricted – you can ask for more to ensure the system's completion. But you are not allowed to compromise on Quality or Time. Now you can have an ongoing dialogue about the additional resources required in order to meet the Quantity, Quality and Time aspects of the project.

The Tri-Level Team Process

Starting with you, the CEO, each manager defines the work of his or her direct reports the next level down. I highly recommend doing this in tri-level team meetings. For example, in a five-level organization, the top tri-level team is composed of the CEO, the VPs and the directors. This is the first step in cascading the strategy down through your organization and having all of your employees "wash it down and then wash it back up" (see figure 7, page 53) to ensure that they clearly understand their work. Each tri-level links to the next tri-level down with two overlapping levels. This creates the most effective message chain.

Think of the effectiveness of having your top three levels (in a five-level organization) meet to discuss and clarify the work of the organization. Your vice presidents and directors hear first-hand, as a team, what you want to accomplish. Any potential mistranslation of strategic issues can be cleared up on the spot. No question should lack an answer, because the CEO is in the room. Best advice and dialogue should reign supreme.

In this meeting, each member of the tri-level team, starting with the CEO, and followed by the VP and each director, presents his or her role and the accountabilities and authorities they have to get work done. It is easy for the CEO to see whether they understand their strategy and whether the work has been planned and aligned sensibly. Team members can challenge, clarify, learn and get aligned behind the strategy. After this tri-level meeting, they should be able to tell a clear story in the subsequent tri-level team meetings that they lead at lower levels as they cascade the strategy and accountabilities farther down the organization.

The same rules of engagement apply at all tri-level meetings. Respectful dialogue should flow both up and down the hierarchy. Employees are accountable for giving their manager and their manager's manager their best advice. Managers have to listen respectfully to best advice. No question should remain unanswered, since there should be no question that cannot be answered when the manager-once-removed is present.

Directors: Linchpins of the Organization

Getting the roles right at the director level is vital to executing your strategy. The directors, located in the structure between the vice presidents and the managers, are the linchpins of a successful organization. Their work requires the translation of their vice president's strategies into operational work for the VP's managers to implement. Figure 31 shows the integrating power of the directors, who, in a five-level organization, are the only level who are members of each tri-level.

Here's how that looks.

1. In the CEO's tri-level team, the directors are the most junior role. They hear first-hand what the CEO wants and can ask for clarification of any issues they perceive with the strategy.

2. Each director then attends the tri-level meeting headed by his or her vice president. The VP clarifies, aligns and integrates the work of the division. The directors play the role of integrator, this time vertically. They create the implementation plans that move the functional strategies created by their VPs into a plan of action. Managers are the most junior in this tri-level team. They have the opportunity to clarify and connect to the work,

challenging their manager-once-removed (the VP) for clarity about their work.

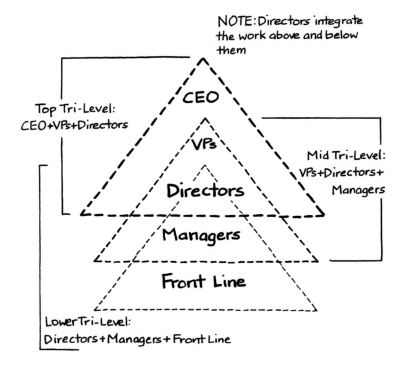

Figure 31: Directors integrate the work above and below them.

3. The directors then lead their own tri-level team meeting with their direct report managers and their front-line employees. The directors, well versed in the strategy, through attending two previous tri-level meetings, now engage the bottom two levels of the organization in implementation/planning discussions. Directors hear first-hand the challenges and blockers to successful implementation. These director tri-level teams are highly operational and focused on delivery. The definitions of roles, accountabilities and authorities are much more black and white. The members of these tri-levels talk about how to get their work done better, faster, cheaper. Directors are the link to this

transactional world of implementation. They can relate, to their direct reports and DRoRs (direct reports-once-removed), the strategy that they themselves learned in the CEO tri-level, where they were the most junior level. This ensures alignment. All the wood is behind the arrowhead, and it is all linked back to the top of the company and the strategy.

Bottom line: none of this works effectively unless:

1. A core function has been chosen.

2. Levels of work have been defined and all prefix titles (additional levels) have been removed.

3. The role of each employee has been defined.

Defining the Work Is Ongoing and Iterative

I sometimes find that managers do the hard work of defining the roles and work of their direct reports but pay scant attention to it afterwards, thinking their task is over. They fail to do the hard work of the craft of executive management. Organizations are living organisms made up of human beings who are ever growing and changing. The work of the organization never ceases to evolve and adapt in the face of competition and changing market and regulatory environments. Technological improvements destroy the value of existing processes, allowing employees to do more with less, or do on their own what used to require the services of sister functions. Change is never-ending in our modern world. Roles must constantly adapt and evolve to keep up. Your role definitions must be living documents that you continually update and adjust in dialogue with your team to reflect the current reality of work in your organization.

We have come full circle in this chapter, from a repudiation of the fake empowerment fad to an understanding of the real, enduring empowerment that releases employees to do their best work – because they have clearly defined roles in which they can use their professional judgment to make decisions about how to get work done.

Employees need not only clarity about their role but also the authority and discretion to actually make the decisions required to be successful in their role. Accountability is one thing – authority or discretion in the role is everything. The next CEO management principle addresses this challenge.

Action Steps

1. What is the state of role definitions in your organization?
   a. Check your own.
   b. Check two of your direct reports' role definitions.
   c. Check two of their direct reports' role definitions.

(5 in total)

_____

_____

_____

_____

_____

2. What did you find? Perfection or opportunity? Remember, you manage 250+ employees. You are accountable to ensure that they are clear on their role and accountabilities.

_____

_____

3. Redraft your role using the role definition form as shown in this chapter. (See figures 25 and 27–30.)

_____

_____

_____

4. How will you use the tri-level model to align the strategy and work of your organization?

_____

_____

_____

Executive Summary

1. To create energy and empowerment among large numbers of employees, you need to clarify their roles and the work they are accountable to do. If employees are not clear about what is expected of them, they will spin and churn.

2. Defining the roles of all your employees is an act of defining and clarifying your strategy in dialogue with your employees.

3. The concept of tri-level teams is a tool to enable you to align the work of your organization.

4. Tri-level teams enable best advice to become a habit.

CHAPTER EIGHT

CEO Management Principle #5: Manage Your Organization's Lateral Relationships

Let's recap the principles covered so far.

Principle #1:	Create Your Strategy
Principle #2:	Choose Your Organization's Functional Structure
Principle #3:	Level the Organization
Principle #4:	Define the Work

Now we come to principle #5: *Manage Your Organization's Lateral Relationships*.

How dare you not integrate the work of your organization!

So far, the CEO management principles have clarified work in functional silos. Now you have to bind everything together to ensure that all of the work of your organization is integrated. You do this by managing the cross-functional work of the organization, which is the accountability of you and your executive team. You cannot just hope that the executives you hire will get along with one another and that each function will work smoothly with the others. You need to manage them and hold them accountable to do so. Mastering principle #5 will enable you to do this.

Let's look at an example.

Joan Watson had been challenged before in her role as a CEO, but not like this. Her latest promotion had made her the CEO of a national retailer. After four months in the role, she was fed up with how her executive team bickered and fought. Talk about a silo mentality! She had never seen it so bad in a company.

"What on earth have I taken on?" she asked herself.

She estimated that 75% of the value the company created for its customers was in cross-functional value chain processes. Take the flyer that her company regularly put out: Marketing, Merchandising, IT, and Store Operations all fought and blamed each other for the failure of the flyer process to promote sufficient footsteps into the store, achieve targeted sales and build customer interest and passion. It was a real battleground. Joan had seen it before, but enough was enough. She called her executives to a meeting to solve the issue.

She named Merchandising accountable for the process.

"You are accountable for the entire flyer process; the flyer is a corporate asset, and I want you to treat it this way. If there are issues, you are accountable to fix them. You others – IT, Marketing, Store Operations – you will work to provide services to Merchandising. You have the appropriate authorities for yourselves to provide advice and audit pricing, and to help coordinate the work. I am going to hold each of you accountable to work effectively and supportively together. If I don't see this, I'll be talking to you about it!"

Cooperation and integration of work on the flyer increased in efficiency and effectiveness over the next six months. Joan kept a close eye on things and intervened swiftly if she saw an issue between any of her direct reports. The flyer program went from strength to strength.

When Executives Fail to Manage Lateral Relationships

The challenge of managing lateral relationships increases as a company grows in levels. A three-level organization, in which all of the employees and processes are contained and report to the same manager, requires no special treatment. This manager coordinates and integrates all of the work.

It is when an organization evolves to four-plus levels that the challenges of lateral integration start. At four levels, the structure creates the first true silos, with employees reporting to function heads and no longer to the CEO. This is when managers and their employees can start to fight and become territorial.

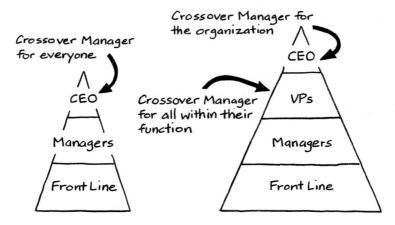

Figure 32: The crossover manager.

It is up to you to integrate this cross-functional work and stamp out any silo infighting. If you don't, your employees may get caught in the crossfire, and that is not fair to them. If you don't, your employees' energy will be stifled and their work will be politicized. I used an analogy earlier for what happens when you don't take charge of your company in various areas. It applies here, too. Ignore your accountability to integrate the cross-functional work of your company and your organization will be like 747 flying across the Atlantic with its flaps down. How would you feel if you sat for seven hours on that plane as it wasted fuel and effort grinding through the air? That's how your employees feel after a day at work if you don't manage these issues effectively.

Often employees try to solve these issues by developing personal relationships across functional boundaries. Employees who have been around long enough are able to call in a favour. This can work quite well for longer-term employees who are extroverted and have good persuasion skills. But new employees with no relationships to call on have a much tougher time getting the services they require to deliver their work effectively. Do you really want the organization's success in managing complex, cross-organizational processes to be compromised by an unclear definition of services? Do you want it to be compromised by basing requests for help on relationships rather than accountabilities?

Another challenge is the effective assimilation of Generation Xers and Millennials into your organization. Their interest and expectation is to have three to six (or more) different careers during their lifetime. These highly transitional generations of employees will require structure, accountabilities and clear lateral relationship authorities if you are going to integrate them swiftly and productively into your workforce.

What Is a Lateral Relationship for an Employee?

To manage something you first have to define it, and this is especially true of lateral relationships.

A lateral relationship occurs when two employees must work together in some way to achieve a goal. The two may be at the same level, but not necessarily. A director can be in a position to request a service from a vice president, for example.

In figure 33, manager Mary has delegated a task to one of her direct reports, Ravi. To accomplish this task, Ravi requires a service from another employee, Rita, who reports not to Mary but to Franco, a different manager. Therefore Ravi needs authority to initiate a task with Rita. This authority can be granted only by the crossover manager at the request of Mary and agreed to by the other manager, Franco, who will now hold his employee Rita accountable to provide it.

To initiate tasks, employees throughout the organization require authorities over particular peers across the organization. The fundamental problem with lateral relationships is the tendency not to define, understand or enforce authorities. Without the required

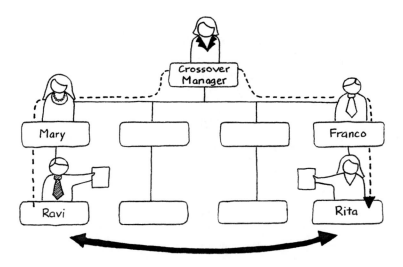

Figure 33: Initiating tasks and the crossover manager.

authority to do their work, employees spin their wheels. What is more, it is blatantly unfair to delegate accountabilities to your employees without giving them the appropriate authority to do their work effectively. Employee effectiveness and trust will be eroded.

Lateral Functional Processes Create 75% of Your Value

Most of the processes in companies for creating value for the customer require departments to work together. As companies grow, this interdependence becomes more complex and requires more and more management time to ensure that it is managed effectively. I estimate that almost 75% of value in large companies is created through processes that cut across functional boundaries. (See figure 34.) If this is accurate, managers have to become extremely skilled at identifying and managing these processes.

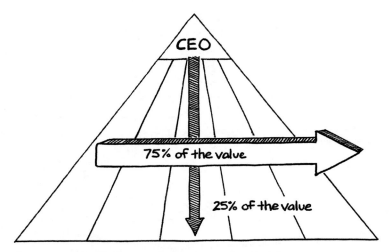

Figure 34: 75% of value comes from cross-functional processes.

Identify the Key Cross-Functional Processes

A practical way to approach the lateral authority issue is to identify the main cross-functional processes of your organization. Once you can define them, identify the handover points, services obtained and resources needed between functions.

You are unlikely to need to go fishing for these. The biggest problems with lateral authorities are most likely your organization's biggest performance problems, too. This is where you'll find the potential battlegrounds in your organization.

I believe that major cross-functional processes should be regarded as a corporate asset in the same way that a store or truck is. You have to have someone accountable for the health and effectiveness of these corporate assets. The value they can spin off, if they are well managed, is too important to ignore. I call this role a process manager. I don't like the word "owner," because it implies possession. Rather, the moment you use the word "manager," the first thing that should drop into your mind is the word "accountability."

What is the process manager accountable for? They are accountable for the integrity and performance of the process, regardless of where in the organization various parts of the process are executed. This manager, with your backup as CEO, will negotiate and confirm all of the functional authorities required to ensure the efficient and effective running of the process. They will then manage the process.

Doing this should clean up potential functional battlegrounds and maximize the value of these corporate assets. As CEO, you must identify and ensure that the major cross-functional value chains are managed in an efficient, effective and trust-enhancing manner.

In terms of the retail flyer (see figure 35), for all of the talk about online purchasing and advertising, most retailers still live and die by the success of their printed mailers listing the latest sales and products. It is a cornerstone of the business, a point of contact with thousands – even millions – of potential customers.

The importance of the mailer to the retail bottom line may surpass any other activity. It certainly is often one of the most expensive. Given this, you would imagine that the work is clearly defined. However, ask those involved, "Who is in charge of the flyer?" and no clear answer emerges. This critical process crosses so many functions that clarifying the accountability and authorities for the process is complex and critical. An unmanaged process becomes a great example of inefficiency and energy-sucking turf wars. Yet it is a critical value chain for retail organizations.

Further Examples

Literally every client I work with has a handful of core cross-functional processes that create the value they deliver to their customers. When I ask, "Who is accountable for the process?" the answer is often fuzzy at best, which means work in these vital systems isn't being done effectively or efficiently. The CEO needs to ensure that this work is integrated and that one individual is held accountable for its success. Figure 36 gives some typical examples.

The Retail Flyer

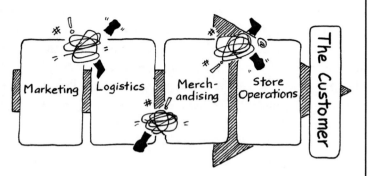

Potential Battlegrounds

- Where your company spins and churns due to lack of organizational clarity and lack of management
- Conflict is a given in this process. Managed well, it contributes to the creativity and productivity of the process

MARKETING

- Builds the flyer theme
- Allocates space
- Can veto products judged not capable of required productivity

LOGISTICS

- Orders
- Delivers merchandise to stores

MERCHANDISING

- Presents merchandise SKUs they judge will meet marketing criteria for flyer

STORE OPERATIONS

- Executes merchandising at the store
- Displays product
- Serves the customer

Figure 35: An example of potential crossover battlegrounds.

Cross-Functional Challenges

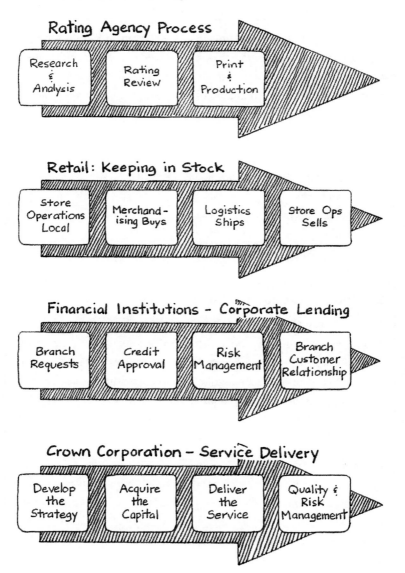

Figure 36: Who is in charge?

What Types of Authority Can You Delegate?

All authority delegated to employees comes from the CEO. In discussion with your direct reports, you, in turn, will grant authorities to each function to enable them to perform their work. Like accountabilities, authorities cascade down through the organization. It is a resource managers can provide to enable their employees to work laterally in the organization.

The types of authority are:

- Advising
- Service getting
- Monitoring
- Coordinating
- Auditing
- Prescribing

Six Types of Lateral Relationships

1. Advising Authority: "Listen to my advice."

You do not want just anyone in the organization giving advice to just anyone else. Advisory authority is for internal experts on matters such as tax, economics or regulations for providing time-sensitive knowledge to managers who require being up to date on that subject. Note: This is the authority to give unsolicited advice. The authority to get advice is a service-getting authority. (See below.)

Example:

In the retail flyer example, the art department may be given advisory authority to Marketing about new printing techniques, changes in the market's colour preferences, advances in graphics applications that could be used and so on. Marketing has to listen to the advice but does not have to put it into practice.

2. Service-getting Authority: "Do this – when I want, if you can."

Employees with service-getting authority can request and get specific services from service providers, who work according to a pre-defined prioritization process. They do not prioritize who gets served when.

Requesters can also specify a delivery deadline. If the service providers cannot meet it, they must provide an estimate of delivery time. The requesting employees can escalate to their own managers if this is not soon enough. If that manager cannot resolve the issue, he or she continues to escalate until the crossover manager resolves it. Requesters are not allowed to badger service providers.

Example:
In a large, six-level investment bank, the Foreign Exchange (FOREX) group has created a new application to help them manage currency swaps. FOREX has the service-getting authority to request that IT place it into production on the server, and requests it for that weekend. IT has a backlog of new systems. They inform FOREX that they cannot meet this deadline but can put the application into production next month. FOREX escalates the matter to their manager, and the two vice presidents of the functions resolve the issue, without involving their CEO, who is the crossover manager.

3. Monitoring Authority: "Conform to my plan or strategy."
An employee who has the accountability for a policy or strategy requires monitoring authority. Other employees must inform the monitor if their actions relate to or affect the policy or strategy. Monitors can ask employees to bring their actions in line when they think the actions are outside these policies or strategies. Employees can refuse a monitor's request if, in their judgment, it would prevent them from getting their work done. If the monitors, as a result, cannot get their own work done, they must escalate to their own manager. The matter can continue to be escalated to the crossover manager, who must resolve the issue.

Example:
Accounting may have monitoring authority over the money spent by Marketing on the retail flyer. They can request that Marketing bring the flyer in on budget but cannot demand it. If Marketing continues to overspend, Accounting can escalate the issue to their manager.

4. Coordinating Authority: "Do this together – when I want, if you can."

An employee with coordinating authority can coordinate the work of specified roles in specified areas but cannot assign actual tasks to employees. The coordinator can call a meeting of lateral employees X, Y and Z to persuade them to act in concert with his or her policy or plan. If they don't act in concert and their lack of cooperation prevents the coordinator from getting assigned work done, the coordinator can escalate the issue to his or her manager. Escalation may continue to the crossover manager, who must resolve the problem.

Example:

A five-level insurance provider is refreshing its desktop computer systems across the company. An IT analyst has coordinating authority with the heads of every department to ensure that they are prepared for the changeover. While this analyst can attempt to persuade departmental directors to follow the plan, she does not have the authority to tell them to do it. Conflicts that cannot be resolved must be escalated to their manager.

5. Auditing Authority (also known as Vetoing Authority): "Conform to my plan or policy even if you disagree."

Auditing authority is similar to monitoring authority in that the auditor has the accountability for a plan or policy, and employees must inform him or her if their actions relate to or affect it. Unlike monitoring authority, auditing authority authorizes the auditor to do more than ask. The auditor can stop employees from continuing to do an action that does not conform to the policy or strategy. The auditor cannot tell other employees to take a certain action, only that they must refrain from taking a certain kind of action. If the employees cannot get their jobs done while complying with the auditor's direction, they can escalate to their own managers. Escalation can continue to the crossover manager, who must resolve the issue.

Auditing is a heavy hammer and should be used judiciously and sparingly. It should not be used if monitoring authority and persuasion suffice.

Example:

A medical testing operations division wants to purchase new equipment and offer a new test to clients. The medical sciences division objects. The problem is one of lateral authorities: Who has the authority to buy new equipment? The CEO clarifies that Operations has the accountability for the types of testing the company provides, but Medical Sciences has auditing authority over the validity of new tests and can veto them.

6. Prescribing Authority: "Do what I tell you to do."

Prescribing authority should be given only where health and safety are at immediate risk. Prescribing authority authorizes the prescriber to tell another employee to do something, and that employee must do it immediately. The employee's manager – not the prescriber – holds him or her accountable for doing it.

Example:

The building security department is accountable for the safety of all employees. If they suspect employees are in danger because of fire, they can clear the entire building. The CEO and the executives must obey immediately.

Common Sense

All employees should be able to ask for advice or help from another employee, without their manager's permission. This is just common sense. And if the request does not consume significant time and resources, they should get the help they request.

Lateral authorities come into play when the request from Ravi (see figure 37) demands significant time or resources from his fellow employee Rita. Unless managed, the informal request can become a significant distraction and prevent the completion of strategic work that Rita's manager Franco is being held accountable to deliver.

Managers need to manage and harbour their resources carefully to ensure that they deliver the work of their function to their manager. Informal requests for help must not undermine the work of the strategic plan. This is often why major projects don't come in on time.

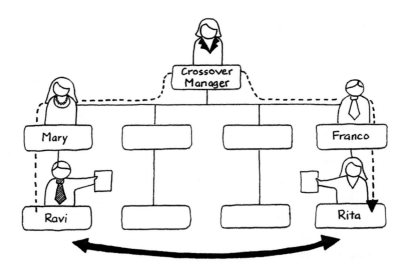

Figure 37: Initiating tasks and the crossover manager.

Lateral Relationships and the Role of Managers

Managers have an important role in managing lateral relationships after you, the crossover manager, have clarified the authorities and assigned single accountability for the process. All managers must hold their direct reports accountable for responding appropriately to legitimate task initiations. Managers must also handle any escalations from their direct reports when they have authority in a lateral relationship but cannot get an adequate response to do their work. They must solve this roadblock by providing other resources, changing the task so it doesn't require support from another department or speaking to the service giver's manager. If all else fails, they must escalate the issue to their manager.

Conflicts and Escalation to the Crossover Manager

As CEO, you are your company's ultimate crossover manager. (See figure 38.) You will need to manage escalation issues raised by your vice presidents. In many cases, the crossover manager is the employees' manager-once-removed (MoR), because all of the managers of the employees involved report to the same person.

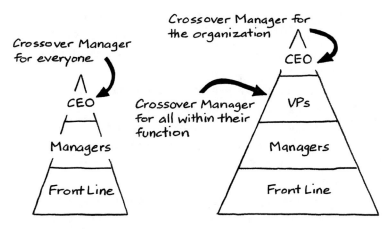

Figure 38: The crossover manager.

The crossover manager originally delegates work to his or her direct reports, who in turn delegate work to their direct reports. When this work is incompatible with work being done by another employee, escalation to the MoR is *required*, for it is the MoR who creates the conflict in the first place by delegating the work, and the MoR is the only person who can resolve and re-prioritize the work while maintaining the context and focus on the key work required to implement the strategy. In the press of accomplishing strategy, MoRs welcome escalation. It enables them to do their work, prioritizing the work of their organization and unblocking or solving issues that enable their employees to get on with the successful implementation of strategy.

Escalation occurs when an employee initiates an agreed-on task with another employee, as in figure 37, in which Ravi initiates a task with Rita. After dialogue, it is clear that any delay is unacceptable and will not allow Ravi to fulfill his accountability to his manager. Rather than spin and churn, they must escalate, i.e., Ravi should inform Rita that he is escalating to his manager, Mary.

There are three basic reasons for escalation. Keep in mind the basic principle at work here, that *no one has the right to cause someone else to fail in their accountability, by compromising their delegated authority.*

- The first reason for escalation is that something in Rita's accountability prevents her from delivering what has been requested. This could be conflicting priorities, a strategy or policy issue or lack of resources
- The second reason is that Rita's accountability to her manager may be challenged by how Ravi handles the task request. Not all service receivers are skilled at making good service requests. After reasonable discussion and attempts to help Ravi be a better task initiator, Rita is obliged to escalate to her manager
- The final reason to escalate would be if Rita simply isn't fulfilling her obligations under the terms of the pre-defined lateral relationship, because of, for example, incompetence, poor communication or bad handling of workload

However, the clarity of roles and authorities ensures that most conflicts can be, and are, resolved at lower levels. The employees' individual managers simply contact one another and discuss the issue. Often a resolution can be found and no further escalation is necessary. This is what you get when you create clarity about roles and authorities: less churn and wasted energy trying to get things done.

Escalation: A Career-Limiting Move?

A lot of employees feel escalating to their manager is the kiss of death to their career. They think that doing so:

- Displays incompetence
- Bothers their manager
- Pressures their manager to deal with a peer or a particularly difficult issue
- Makes them look politically inept

So they hold the issue at their level and get sucked into a frustrating, spinning whirlpool as they try (often valiantly) to obtain the service they require from a non-cooperative division (not managed by their manager). In another example, a Finance person may experience difficulties and frustration because someone in Marketing consistently ignores sending agreed-on data that is required for the quarterly roll-up of divisional results. Or an IT person may have problems because someone hasn't had the time or interest to take a training course on a piece of software and then creates problems with the help desk.

Unless escalation is driven by threats to accountability, and assuming the process is being followed, escalation should not be considered snitching. When escalation is not grounded in account-ability, it is snitching. If you surprise someone by escalating without letting them know, it can become personal. Instead, keep escalation grounded in accountability.

Escalation ought to be seen by everyone in a positive, not a nega-tive light. Escalation makes managers do the work they are supposed to do: prioritizing work and integrating it for the organization. It is blatantly unfair for an employee to be assigned an accountability and not be provided the appropriate authority to get it done.

This Is CEO Work

As CEO, you are the ultimate crossover manager. It's no good asking, "Why can't I get someone else to do this for me?" This is your account-ability as CEO. If you aren't doing this, you aren't doing your job. If you don't appreciate the power of clarifying laterals, you've missed the key to empowering, engaging and energizing your organization.

And if you're not the crossover manager for a core process, then you must identify the position that is the crossover manager. You must then ensure that this person's role definition includes account-ability for the process and the required lateral authorities. Finally, you must ensure that the managers of other functions who participate in executing this core process also have the necessary accountabilities and authorities in their role definitions.

Perhaps the thought of having to hash it out with your direct reports de-energizes you. It's certainly true that unmanaged infighting at the top is debilitating to an organization. But it's nowhere close to as debilitating as it is lower down the organization. It can be nearly impossible for your employees to work efficiently and effectively without extraordinary additional effort and frustration. And then there's the totally unfair Catch-22 position you have put them in. "I want you to do this, but I am not giving you the authority to get it done." Nice play, Mr./Ms. CEO!

You may find it difficult to empathize with these concerns, because you are the only member of your organization who does not require delegated authority to get your work done. You are the ultimate boss. As the initiator of all authority in your organization, you can do as you please. This is a freedom and privilege that nobody else has. Often CEOs take this freedom for granted and forget how limited freedom and choice are for front-line employees. That is why you have to champion the front line and always be vigilant and understanding of how effectively your managers exercise the accountability and authority you delegate to them.

A Word About Discretion

When you delegate an authority to employees, you must allow them to use it and must ensure that they have the freedom to think through and decide what solution fits the outcome they are accountable for. I call this the "discretion to act as they see fit." It doesn't mean that, as manager, you don't provide coaching and support. It does mean that you must step back and give them the space and freedom to act. Your employees probably won't do it the way you think it should be done – but you must not interfere. You may cringe when you see how an employee uses their discretion, but, unless they are heading for an unmitigated disaster, you must trust them to see it through their way. If you don't, they will never really believe that they have the freedom to act on their own.

Work in your organization requires the use of discretion; without discretion, it could be done by a machine. The more discretion you delegate to front-line employees, the more likely they will be to feel respected, value their work and engage effectively and efficiently in executing your strategy,

Generally, the lower you go in an organization, the more managers try to control their employees. This basically squeezes the juice out of employees, which is terrible. It's not the nature of the beast for most managers to let go. They are always afraid that employees will go haywire using the discretion implicit in the authority they are given. But you have to have faith in people.

I cannot emphasize enough how important it is to delegate discretion with the accountabilities that you task to your employees. If you don't, you're not treating employees fairly; you're not trusting them to do the right thing; you're depriving them of growth and learning; you're sucking the energy out of your organization.

If you are concerned that employees will hide behind their accountabilities, don't be. In my experience, employees are more likely to cooperate with requests when they know what they have to do and what they don't.

Here is a good example of the difference delegated discretion can make. One of our clients had a policy that if a customer had a complaint and the bill had to be adjusted, for anything over 50 cents, the lead or manager had to be asked for permission. What happened? People asked … and asked … and asked, and the manager was so overwhelmed, he approved everything. The result was $4 million in adjustments each year.

After a review, the vice president decided that employees should be given more discretion. After all, the employee on the phone, dealing with the customer, probably has the best view of the client's issues and the fairness of their request or complaint. The approval limit was raised so anything higher than $50 was to be escalated to the manager. The effect? Adjustments went from $4 million to $1 million because employees knew exactly whether a customer was entitled to an adjustment. Front-line employees who made those judgment calls thought this was great.

This is one of those classic examples where everyone exclaimed, "Why didn't we do this sooner?"

As a CEO, you need to understand the importance of the right of employees to use discretion in their work, and the energy and engagement multiplier it will become throughout your organization. In the end, it is the use of discretion that transforms your employees' world. It is your accountability to ensure that they have discretion and use it.

I come now to the third time in which I have to warn against giving this work to HR. It's not their work; it's yours and your managers'. Earlier I stressed that creating strategy and implementing it should not be punted to HR. Likewise, don't delegate the accountability for clarifying lateral authorities to HR. If you do, you'll send a clear message to the organization (and to your executive team, in particular) that this work is not important – and they will see it as just that. It is not fair to HR. HR does not have the authority to do this work. If it is given to them, it will be ignored by the line managers and fizzle out. As a result, your organization will never operate at its best. It is your executive management work with your vice presidents to get your head around how you manage the lateral dynamic authorities created for your employees.

How dare you duck this core executive work!

Note that the larger the company and the higher the number of levels, the more challenging and complex it becomes to achieve significant pieces of work. *It must be managed* so that hundreds of your employees can work effectively and efficiently.

How to Clarify Role Relationships

Clarifying lateral role relationships is exacting work. Learning how to work in them may also feel like a lot of fuss over nothing. Resist the temptation to abdicate your executive management work. Getting lateral relationships clear and learning to work with them will prevent problems and make coordination and cooperation much easier. And that will improve productivity and increase your ability to manage large numbers of employees.

To make laterals work, hold regular tri-level meetings. Quarterly tri-level meetings to review progress to plan can be very useful.

Jos Wintermans relates this experience:

"We asked every manager in our company to provide measurements around what was done in their departments. For instance, the cafeteria manager would ask, 'How much food do we consume? How much waste do we generate?' The point of the exercise was to uncover the controls needed to get the work done. Once managers started to dig deeper and really think about how they perform, they would encounter boundaries. These boundaries occurred when someone from another department would hand over product, or data, or information – something required in order to complete their work. Often on receiving this piece of information it would be established that it needed improvements to bring it up to standard so that the next step in the process could be completed. So employee Jack in IT would be forced to spend uncreative time to improve information from employee Joan in Finance.

"This is the essence of the tension in the cross-functional process where managers accept their accountabilities but in order to accomplish their outputs are forced to grade the inputs from other departments. There are inputs, and there are outputs – between the two lies unproductive time to smooth things out. If problems occur on a frequent basis, trust is eroded. If you cannot get the service and quality you require, this is what I call the trustbuster. At some point they don't trust the person to do the right thing anymore, and therefore they work around them."

However, when tri-level meetings occur on a regular quarterly basis, managers have the opportunity to speak frankly to their peers and state, "We need a certain quality (or quantity) of data from you so I'm not forced to spend time to bring it up to standard." The focus here is on improving existing processes to get work done satisfactorily. Elliott Jaques believed this process to be a trust-enhancing methodology.

Wintermans continues, "For example, in order to accept commercial accounts, we needed credit report rating agency ratings, bank statements and other items in order to start doing business with them. Our salespeople would say, 'We've gained 100 accounts this month!' But the credit people who were tasked to set up the account said, 'It's hard to set up, as we don't have this, and we need that.' Everyone pointed fingers at each other, blaming others for their inability to complete their accountabilities.

"We found that quarterly tri-level meetings put a stop to this. Slowly but surely the handover of outputs from one department became less problematic as QQTRs (Quantity, Quality, Timing, Resources) were clearly stated (especially with regard to Quality), delivered and consistently maintained. Once people started getting the hang of it, they were able to figure out where the next level of improvement could come from. This was not always under their control, but came from someone else, who had to improve a service in order to provide a better, smoother output."

It's CEO work to choose the practical cadence of these meetings to suit your business, always taking into account geographic challenges and the pressures of your business.

From Battle Zones to Free Trade Zones

As the top manager of your organization, you must manage the use of authority within it. Remember, all authority in your company flows from you, the CEO. When you started the work on authorities, you decided with your executive team the authorities you would delegate to each reporting function. You need to be persistent in your insistence that these authorities are efficiently and effectively delegated downwards through your organization all the way to the front line.

If you abdicate this accountability, your employees will pay the price. If untrusting and ineffectual managers delegate tasks and limit the use of discretion, your organization will experience churn, wasted time, frustration and employee disengagement. In stark contrast, when you manage your organization's lateral relationships, the battle zones become free trade zones, and cooperation replaces cacophony.

Action Steps

1. Consider how much time and attention you and your managers pay to integrating the work of your organization. How well does your team work together? Is the organization siloed? Are there turf wars?

2. Identify three key organizational cross-functional processes involving lateral relationships. Remember, these are corporate assets.
   a. How effectively are they being managed?
   b. Is one individual accountable for each process?
   c. How effectively do the different divisions accountable to contribute to the cross-functional process work together?

3. Choose one cross-functional process. Draw the process, highlighting the gaps between each function.
   a. In the highlighted space, name the authorities that you have granted each division to enable them to get their accountabilities in the process completed efficiently and effectively.
   b. What opportunities for increased clarity do you find?
   c. Who has the overall accountability and the required authority to manage this cross-functional process?

Executive Summary

1. To create energy and empowerment among large numbers of employees, you need to clarify their role and the work they're accountable to do. Also ensure that they have the appropriate authorities to get their work done. If you do not ensure that authorities are clear and usable, you are not being fair to your employees.

2. Identify and integrate the work of the key cross-functional processes of your organization that deliver value to your customer.

3. If you ignore your accountability to integrate the work of your organization, your employees will spin and churn inefficiently and ineffectively as they try to accomplish their work.

4. This is your CEO management work. It is not HR's.

5. Ensure that escalation happens. Otherwise you won't know what your organization's issues are.

6. Clean up the battlegrounds. Make them free trade zones!

CHAPTER NINE

CEO Management Principle #6: Build the Required Talent

Here are the principles we've covered so far:

Principle #1:	Create Your Strategy
Principle #2:	Choose Your Organization's Functional Structure
Principle #3:	Level the Organization
Principle #4:	Define the Work
Principle #5:	Manage Your Organization's Lateral Relationships

Now we come to principle #6: *Build the Required Talent.*

Jos Wintermans started to implement the CEO management principles at CTAL (now Canadian Tire Financial Services) twenty-five years ago. The principles have been followed by all four succeeding CEOs. The company set out very purposefully to build the talent required for the future (principle #6). They created an impressive cadre of talent internally, added to it externally and nurtured it within the company. This talent pool has enabled the company to successfully execute complex strategies year after year. Most impressively, while doing this, CTFS has supplied at least fourteen senior executives to Canadian Tire (its $10-billion parent company) with little loss of momentum.

CTFS's experience demonstrates what happens when a company has a consistent, concentrated talent development process in which realistic assessment occurs and capable talent is grown and promoted and held to account for effective performance.

As Wintermans comments, "I don't think I am a better picker of talent than other people, but the seven CEO management principles put the emphasis on capability. Following the principles can more easily expose managers who do not possess that capability. I never ended up with a lot of deadwood, as we just kept weeding it out. My direct reports then started doing the same thing and the process became a self-fulfilling prophecy. Once you are out in the open with this accountability, nobody can hide and talent building really starts in earnest."

How dare you not build talent capable of implementing your strategy!

Jim Collins famously wrote, in *Good to Great*, that CEOs need to get the right people on the bus and worry about getting them into the right seats later.[27] It's a great metaphor, except for one small problem: he never says how you know who is right for the bus and how you know who is right for the various seats in order to excel. You don't want to put people into a role who overpower it. They will end up getting bored. Nor do you want to promote people to a higher-level position that overwhelms them. They will flounder and fail to complete the work of the role.

It seems that there is much more to this "getting the right people on the bus" than Collins let on. In your initial pass at levelling your organization and defining the work of the roles, you will have gained ground in determining the type of seats you have on the bus. For example, you may know that you need certain director-level operational roles in your five-level organization. Find people who truly fit these roles and can work effectively in them, roles that stretch them enough to grow and be engaged but not so much that they are overwhelmed and sink.

How Do You Judge Capability?

Did you ever meet someone from a vendor or a partner firm and find yourself surprised by his or her job title?

"That's a vice president?" you think. "He doesn't seem capable enough to be an executive!"

You may muse for a while and then move on, deciding that his company must be unaware of what vice presidents really do.

Or perhaps you can recall going to a dinner party with pre-arranged seating meant to separate couples, and within five minutes you know you're going to be bored for the whole evening. It's not so much that you're a snob as that your tablemates simply don't have much of interest to say. Meanwhile, your significant other is at the other end of the table, laughing with *her* tablemates all evening.

Maybe you have run into an immigrant working at a menial job and quickly realize, even through a language barrier, that this person could do a lot more if given the chance. You were fooled at first, but your insight saw past the janitor's uniform.

What you are doing, in all of these examples, is subconsciously and subjectively assessing someone's capability. You cannot help doing this. You do it every time you meet someone. You ask and answer the question, "How smart are they?" and you do this repeatedly.

I suggest that, when you're determining the required talent for a role, you formalize this subjective process of judgment. As CEO, you should continually assess the kind of thinking that you require at each level in your organization to achieve your strategy. What you need is a way to assess the people who might fit these roles. The four components of employee capability will help you to do this. Let's have a look at them.

The Four Components of Employee Capability

An employee's capability to be successful in a role depends on the following four components:

1. Their cognitive capacity: their ability to handle the complexity of the work delegated to them by their manager.

2. The knowledge and skills required to do the work.

3. Their valuing of and commitment to the role and the work.

4. Their temperament (the absence of any deep-seated behaviour or personality traits that could derail their ability to be effective in the role).

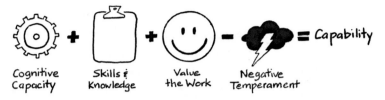

Cognitive Capacity + Skills & Knowledge + Value the Work − Negative Temperament = Capability

Figure 39: What employees need to succeed.

Of these four, cognitive capacity is the most important to get right, because it is the one you can do little to change. You can grow an employee's skills and knowledge through training, education and job mentoring. You can energize employees by giving them work that they value. But there is little you can do to change how well an employee thinks. It is what it is. Their thinking may evolve over time, but it usually is resistant to evolving faster than what is natural for the person.

1. *Cognitive Capacity*

Getting the cognitive capacity right by level is critical. It is the key that enables managers and employees to thrive with the level of complexity of work delegated at that level. I am talking about how you create successful employees in successful organizations. You need to match the employees' capability to the level of work in the role. This is why the first five CEO management principles are so important: they set the organization up to manage talent fairly and strategically. You can see in figure 40 that different thinking is required at different levels of your organization. As a result, different capabilities for different levels of work are also needed.

I regard cognitive capacity as the key management competency. If managers or employees cannot think effectively to solve the complexity of issues delegated to them in their role,

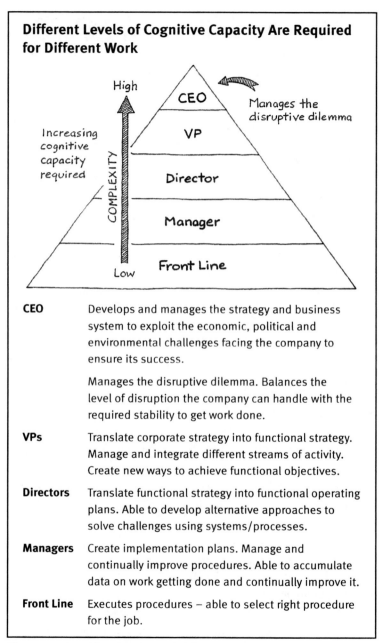

Different Levels of Cognitive Capacity Are Required for Different Work

CEO   Develops and manages the strategy and business system to exploit the economic, political and environmental challenges facing the company to ensure its success.

         Manages the disruptive dilemma. Balances the level of disruption the company can handle with the required stability to get work done.

VPs   Translate corporate strategy into functional strategy. Manage and integrate different streams of activity. Create new ways to achieve functional objectives.

Directors   Translate functional strategy into functional operating plans. Able to develop alternative approaches to solve challenges using systems/processes.

Managers   Create implementation plans. Manage and continually improve procedures. Able to accumulate data on work getting done and continually improve it.

Front Line   Executes procedures – able to select right procedure for the job.

Figure 40: Cognitive capacity and different types of work.

it devalues the use of their skills and knowledge. This capacity cannot be harnessed effectively by people who are overwhelmed in their role. You need to hire it right in the first place and not over-promote in cases in which the cognitive capacity for the role is not there.

2. *Skills and Knowledge*
Unlike cognitive capacity, skills and knowledge can be coached. The employee's manager should know clearly what skills and knowledge are required to enable the employee to function effectively in the role. This is the manager's decision and not a mechanical reference to a set of competencies. It's part of a manager's ability to add value.

Watch out for this trap: Often a long-time employee has deep skills and knowledge in a role. They naturally exude confidence and insight in their work. Managers often mistranslate this high level of skill and knowledge as high cognitive ability. It could be, but often it is not; it is a demonstration of historical expertise. Check it by presenting a future-based scenario with the solution dependent on some longer-term future-based strategies. See what you get as an answer.

3. *Valuing of and Commitment to the Work*
This is often underestimated or misunderstood as a motivator and driver of performance. Think about it, though. It measures how much employees *love* their work. Employees who value their role are full of pep and vigour, happy to be in the role and with what they do. Be sure you pay attention to this and match your employees to the type of work they appreciate and value. Doing the opposite will produce dismal, grudging, unhappy performance, not what you want around your company.

4. *Temperament*
As for the fourth element, employees must be free of any noticeably difficult personality issues. They don't need to have a particular personality, nor do they need to be self-actualized;

they simply must not have any entrenched psychological or personality traits that disrupt normal behaviour, for example, deep-seated anger that leads to out-of-control outbursts that could threaten the social and psychological safety of their peers.

Be careful here. Poor communications skills do not equal negative temperament. I am talking about serious derailers of a psychological nature that are not in a manager's purview to solve. Call Human Resources. This kind of issue can be dealt with only by the employee assistance program. Managers do not have the skills to deal with these types of behavioural pathologies.

How Managers Evaluate the Capability of Direct Reports

Managers hold an accurate subjective view of their direct reports' effectiveness. I have seen this consistently in my clients, even at the start of an engagement. They draw their conclusions from their experience and interactions with their direct reports. They say things like:

- "I have to tell this person what I want two or three times before they understand. Then when they actually do what I want, it is delivered late and I am underwhelmed with the result"
- "When I delegate work to these employees, they pick up the nuances of the issue very fast and come back with a solution that is innovative and just what was needed"
- "I like their use of discretion and judgment"

You can make these judgments of your team right now. If I asked you to take a piece of paper and rank your direct reports from the highest capability to the lowest, you could do it immediately and accurately. I have been asking my clients to do this for over two decades, and the results always stand up when I challenge them.

You can do this because, as you manage people, you get a feel for how "big" or "small" they are in their roles. You see how they relate to their peers, whether they hold their own with them, how they impress them and help them solve their issues. You see how they add value to the work of their direct reports. You do this naturally. (See figure 41.) Remember the discussion about creating the right-sized sandbox in principle #4, *Define the Work*. Understanding and using the four components of capability will help you define work much more effectively.

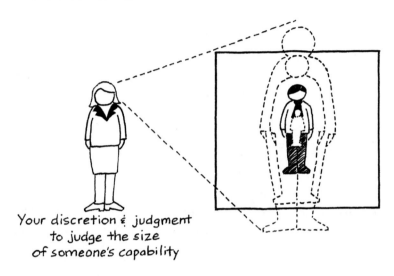

Your discretion & judgment
to judge the size
of someone's capability

Figure 41: How "big" an employee needs to be to fit a role.

A Brick or a Beach Ball?

Managers can evaluate employees by asking themselves a simple question: Is this person a brick or a beach ball? In this analogy, employees must stay at water level to do their work. Bricks need constant energy from you to keep them from sinking. Consider, for example, a vice president who thinks like a director-level manager. This VP lacks the basic thinking capability to do the work you delegate. He drags you down into his organization because you have to constantly work to keep him afloat. Bricks frustrate their managers and their employees. Left in place, this vice president will get rid of any effective directors and replace them with people who should be managers but are given an inflated title. Bricks pull their organizations down to their level of capability.

A beach ball is just the opposite. Watch children at the pool trying to sink their beach ball. No matter how hard they struggle to keep it under water, it keeps popping up. This is exactly what you experience with over-capable employees. They are underwhelmed in their current role and keep popping up into higher-level work that matches how they think. Over-capability in a role may sound like a good thing, but the incumbent will become bored and disillusioned and unmotivated if left in a wrong-fitting role for too long. Beach balls want to do work that fits them.

What is critical is fitting the employee to the role. When you get it right, work feels natural to them. It excites them. Quite simply, it "fits." As their manager, you're not forced to spend time keeping them afloat. You have got it right and in doing so will have a highly energized employee keen to do highly effective work.

As a CEO, this is your strategic challenge. Whatever number of employees you have, you need to use the CEO management principles to optimize the fit-to-role of every employee in your organization.

Handling "Misfits"

When the Role is Too Big and the Work Too Complex

In your assessment of your direct reports' capability, you may discover that one or more cannot do the thinking necessary to translate your strategy down to the next levels: they just don't have the cognitive capacity. This capacity seems to evolve at a rate that is natural to the person, given the right environment and stimuli. As mentioned above, you cannot coach people to greater cognitive capacity. Direct reports who lack this capacity will shrink their role down to something they can manage, destroying value and blocking potential executives at lower levels.

Unless you want to sacrifice your organization's efficiency, you will have to find a smaller job for them or let them go.

When the Role Is Too Small and the Work Too Easy

It's obvious what to do when you have employees who lack the level of capability for their roles – move them out. But what about employees with too much capability? The accepted wisdom is that you've done your job because someone who has capability to burn will run through their work quickly and efficiently. Often this is true, but the more concerning issue is that they may become bored. The work is too small. Worse, the manager now must compete with employees who think they can do the manager's job.

This is a recipe for organizational dysfunction. Bored employees start challenging their managers, who respond ineffectually. The employees push back, harder, out of boredom or amusement. Matters escalate into a full-blown disorder, all because of boredom. Not to mention the more complex projects these employees might initiate on their own that could counter your strategy.

Don't think you can solve these employees' boredom by simply giving them more work. They will just get bored faster and become even more disgruntled. They need bigger work, not more work.

So what should you do about them? They need to be promoted – if worthy – to more challenging roles with greater complexity in the work. If there is no place to go, the manager must have a frank talk with the over-capable employee about the situation. He or she may choose to stay, but the manager must be aware of issues that may arise down the road.

What Happens When the Fit Is Right?

One IT vice president with whom I worked just could not get her team of director-level direct reports to stop surprising her with bad news. Key projects were coming in late and over budget. Her managerial judgment was that two of her seven direct reports just did not have the capability to be effective in their roles. She thought the other five did, but weren't performing well.

That little bit of under-capability was bringing down not just their department but the entire team.

The VP put off making the hard call until finally she had had enough. She let the two under-capable performers go, replacing them with two highly experienced hires whom she judged as capable at the very top of the director level.

What a difference! Like the proverbial tiny bit of yeast leavening the whole loaf, her two new hires brought new life into the entire team. Their mindset gave new confidence to their longer-serving peers, who started working closer to the level of their capability. Best advice shot through the roof. Meetings were energy-charged and energy-charging. The new hires started pushing back when the VP's CIO boss came down and tasked the lower levels directly.

When you get really great capability on your team, capability that fits-to-role at the high end, these employees are not going to just sit there and take it. They will force great processes and build confidence and trust through the organization – and deliver results.

Stop Inflicting Dolts on Your Employees!

Jan's manager, John, taught her nothing – even hindered her from achieving her work, dragging her potential performance down. John spent his time engaged in negative, wasteful, defensive routines. Jan, feeling completely suppressed as John struggled to maintain control and the status quo, reached the conclusion: "My manager is a dolt!" and very nearly told him that. It was almost a career-ending experience.

If you want to screw up your employees' energy, put someone in charge who lacks the cognitive ability to contribute properly. It is your accountability as CEO to build an organization in which employees don't have dolts as managers but managers who enable them to achieve great value. Think about the misery and lost energy that you cause if you allow wrong-fit managers to suffocate your employees.

Managers must feel like "real managers" to their direct reports, managers who truly add value to their work. Managers must think differently – more powerfully and with greater sophistication than their direct reports – to set context for their reports' work. They must see issues, insights and long-term implications that the direct reports cannot see. The employees should feel that their manager's thinking enables them to handle a greater degree of complexity, to weave scenarios together to add value and provide enriching insights. They should feel that their manager can teach them and stretch them, and generally cannot be out-thought by them.

This larger capability and different thinking style creates trust. It enriches the employees' work and enables them to accomplish goals that they never thought possible. This relationship between manager and direct reports is the key to executive success and requires the manager's continued attention.

Managers who cannot do this must be removed from their role, especially when they are at the executive level where they can do greater damage. Put a replacement in who does add value and watch employees become re-energized. Your employees will thank you and add the rejoinder, "What took you so long?"

Imagine what your organization would be like if all managers added value to the work of their employees. Think of how much more your employees could accomplish towards your strategic goals.

This accountability demonstrates the importance of executive management over leadership. The charismatic leader whose chief skill as CEO is pumping up employees' emotions at meetings will find this engagement short-lived if the employees go back to the day-to-day reality of being managed by a dolt.

Studies show that the number-one reason people leave organizations is the quality of their relationship with their immediate manager.[28] Build an organization that removes this reason. All of your employees deserve the best – including your direct reports.

Don't Shore Up Overwhelmed Managers

Of course, some managers erroneously think that capability is a guideline and not a hard and fast rule. They favour this person or that, putting them into roles where their thinking styles are insufficient to the tasks. When these overwhelmed employees flounder, the manager starts to shore them up with assistant managers (title creep) who do what the managers should be doing.

This never works. Managers without sufficient capability to carry out their roles effectively stifle and kill organizations. Leaving them in place only leads to organizational dysfunction and distrust of management. You must remove managers who cannot do the work before they do too much damage. Dallying doesn't just destroy shareholder value; it can damage these managers' self-confidence because they can never effectively complete the work they are assigned to do.

Hold Managers Accountable for Outputs

If you want an organization that is recognized for how it continually builds great capability, enforce one simple policy: *All managers are accountable for the outputs of their employees*. There can be absolutely no exceptions. As CEO, you are accountable to hold your managers accountable for all of their employees to work effectively on the tasks they are delegated.

Managerial accountability for the outputs of their direct reports kills Teflon management dead. This policy is both trust-enhancing and ensures that capability is continually developed throughout your organization. Managers who hold their direct reports accountable for their outputs have to point the finger at themselves, not others, when there is any failure to deliver. They must ensure that they have highly capable employees who can do the work delegated to them. They need to coach and develop their direct reports to higher levels of capability because this is a required norm of management throughout the organization.

If some of their direct reports are incapable of doing this work, they should be removed from their role on the team or be reassigned. Employees with higher capability and potential should replace them so you can build a team of higher capability to successfully and effectively deliver the outputs that you delegate to them. As CEO, you need to ensure that your managers throughout your company are continually increasing the capability of their team.

Talent Building:
The Manager-once-Removed Process

To grow talent in your organization, you need to use the manager-once-removed process, as seen in figure 42.

The manager-once-removed (MoR) is accountable to acquire and develop the talent and careers of direct reports-once-removed (DRoRs): the direct reports of their own direct reports. Managers are accountable to coach their direct reports to maximize their capability in their current role. MoRs are accountable to mentor their direct reports-once-removed in their careers and grow the talent capable of replacing their own direct reports, or provide these employees with other opportunities for career advancement in other parts of the company.

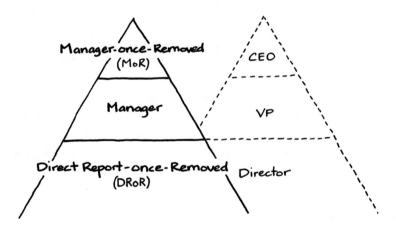

Figure 42: Manager-once-removed, manager, direct report-once-removed.

Managers often challenge us, saying it is their job – not the MoR's – to develop their own replacements and coach their direct reports in their careers. While there is no harm in managers taking an interest in their direct reports' careers, it is the MoR who determines who that manager's successor will be, and who will be the MoR's direct reports. Also, the MoR is the more senior manager, with broader experience and perspective and a greater understanding of the capability requirements of the organization for future talent requirements and possible career opportunities.

The manager's true role is to coach and maximize their direct report's capability in their current role. The MoR will solicit best advice from the manager on the direct report's capability. The MoR may ask the manager to develop certain skills in one of their employees as part of the MoR's career development plan for the direct report-once-removed. Employees get to talk to a senior manager who spends an hour talking about their career potential and creates a plan to pursue it. They love the process.

Annual Mentoring Meeting

At least annually, meet individually with each of your DRoRs for a mentoring conversation in which you ask them how things are going and what they like and don't like about their job or the processes they manage. Help them understand where you see them going in the corporation. This conversation has four main components:

1. "What are your ambitions?"

2. "Let me tell you about the capabilities our organization is looking for."

3. "I see you being able to get there here" or "I don't see you being able to get there here."

4. "Let's work out a plan for your career development."

This is done in dialogue, the respectful give-and-take that is necessary in all crucial conversations. This lets you take on the tough discussion about their careers. Avoiding these conversations is a disservice to the organization and the employee. MoRs must be truthful to their DRoR regarding their future potential. It is unfair and unacceptable not to tell the truth to an employee with career expectations that are unrealistic and cannot be met in your organization. By telling them the truth, you give them the choice to stay or leave. It creates an honest culture in which employees know where they stand and are prevented from wasting years on the wrong rung of a career ladder.

You and your managers do this work. Your managers are also MoRs. The strength and credibility of great talent development work occurs when it is done by line managers. You become the role model for your organization. You mentor; you plan with your DRoRs; you tell some of your DRoRs that they do not have the potential to go to the next level; you plan the next step in their careers. HR will provide supporting documentation and help administer the process. You drive the building of great capability in your company. It is your work.

Developing DRoRs

Sometimes you will want to develop DRoRs for other roles in your organization. This may require pulling them from their current position and placing them in other roles to expand their experience or to test their readiness. This causes a conflict of interest in career development for managers, because it means they may lose the best employees on their team. Your direct report may protest that she cannot meet her QQTRs (Quantity, Quality, Timing, Resources) without this resource. You will need to adjust this QQTR in fairness to your direct report. It is the CEO's accountability to balance the needs of business units with the strategic needs of the organization, including developing the talent pipeline. Work it out in dialogue with your direct report.

The Right People in the Right Roles = Big Benefits

As you have seen, each CEO principle builds to the next. Every CEO management principle we've looked at so far leads to this critical principle of talent management. We have talked about creating a clean clear structure with clearly defined roles, accountabilities and authorities that enable your employees to get their work done. To make your organization really sing, you have to fill these roles with the people who will excel in them. Get the right people in the right seats on the bus.

Take this principle seriously, because without the required capability, your organization will plane at best. Nothing great will happen unless you get fit-to-role right in all roles. Once that is done, you need the last CEO management principle to help set your organization's energy, talent and results on fire. This final principle highlights the importance, for managers, of consistently using a simple set of general management practices.

Action Steps

1. List your team of direct reports. Now rank them according to your judgment of their capability.

_____

_____

_____

_____

2. Can all of them do the thinking required to translate your strategy to the next level?

_____

_____

3. If you could have anyone on your top team, who would they be and why? Why would it not be the same as the direct reports who are with you right now?

_____

_____

4. What is stopping you from putting this team together?

_____

_____

Executive Summary

1. Fit-to-role: Match employee capability to work that they value and challenges them. This will make your organization sing.

2. How dare you inflict on employees managers who cannot add value? Allowing this kills employee engagement.

3. Use your judgment and discretion to determine employee capability. Trust yourself on this. Your determination will be correct.

4. Do not tolerate bricks or beach balls in your organization.

5. Use the manager-once-removed process to develop your employees' careers and talent.

CHAPTER TEN

CEO Management Principle #7: Make It All Happen with Effective Management

So far, we have covered six of the seven CEO management principles:

Principle #1:	Create Your Strategy
Principle #2:	Choose Your Organization's Functional Structure
Principle #3:	Level the Organization
Principle #4:	Define the Work
Principle #5:	Manage Your Organization's Lateral Relationships
Principle #6:	Build the Required Talent

And now we come to the seventh and last principle: *Make It All Happen with Effective Management.*

How dare you manage without a consistent set of management practices!

Early in my career I worked in the food business. My first role as a manager was to manage a team of five people in installing a chocolate manufacturing plant. I progressed to managing ten employees lighting ovens and forty employees packing biscuits. Then I moved to retail, where I managed a series of store departments with fifteen to forty employees in each one.

I found all of the above to be tough work: I had my good days, but as a young manager I was naive and clumsy. I received no formal training, just some good coaching, but after that, I was on my own. Typical of other stories of managers' early careers, I learned by trial and error.

I'll never forget the day I was introduced to the set of management practices described in this chapter. Reading them for the first time, I realized what I had been missing – what had kept me from becoming a really effective manager.

It made me angry. I was thirty-two years old at the time. Why hadn't I discovered these before? Adopting them enabled me to completely settle down and transform my level of effectiveness as a manager. The eleven practices described in this chapter enabled me to become clear and consistent in how I managed my employees while building a highly engaged and capable team. Not bad! My confidence soared, and my accomplishments as a manager became much more significant. I felt anchored and professional for the first time.

Management Makes It Happen

This last principle pulls everything together. Good management makes it happen, and everything happens because of good management. We have talked at length about structuring and organizing work. But without management that reinforces policies, sets performance goals and holds direct reports to account for their work, forethought, planning and preparation will fail.

As discussed earlier in this book, as CEO, you are accountable to align and integrate the work of your organization. You are also accountable to manage the managers of your organization, ensuring they are working within policies that you set such as "managers are accountable for the outputs of their employees" and "a manager of managers will ensure that all of his or her direct reports can add value to the work of those they manage." Remember, the higher up you go in the organization, the more management matters over leadership to effectively manage and engage large numbers of employees. Your employees must be managed consistently up, down and across the organization.

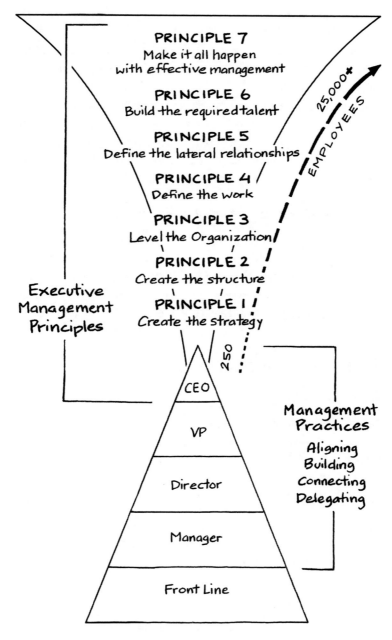

Figure: 43: The complete CEO.

Here is an opportunity for you, the CEO, to raise your company to the next level.

The eleven practices are categorized in the lower half of the Complete CEO diagram (see figure 43) as Aligning, Building, Connecting, and Delegating and are described in full below. Making these practices part of your management DNA is the final step in the CEO management principles and will transform your company. The previous six CEO management principles set up the possibility for great management to occur. It is up to you to make this happen through the management practices.

The Eleven General Management Practices

Let's look more closely at the eleven management practices for managing direct reports. Your challenge is how to use these practices with all of your managers to reinforce what you and your executive team want done. Your management team needs to be able to consistently and professionally engage your 250 to 25,000+ employees.

Following are the practices, with some comments.

The Management Practices

1. Context Setting

Clearly communicating the environment surrounding the task, role or meeting, where it fits in the plan and any relevant situational information.

2. Team Planning

The development of plans for major tasks through dialogue and best advice with the team as a whole. Team planning is tied to the accountability of the outputs of others.

3. Team Building

The practice of holding regular and frequent meetings with your immediate direct reports to build their ability to work with you and with each other. Team building provides an opportunity for managers to set context and plan with their team.

4. Task Assignment

Delegating tasks to your direct reports for them to solve, with clearly stated QQTRs.

5. Task Adjustment

No plan survives first contact. Changes and adjustments need to be made to QQTRs.

6. Monitoring

Keeping track of what direct reports produce so the manager can assess how effectively his or her direct reports are working at the tasks they were given to do.

7. Coaching

Normal, day-to-day process by which managers reinforce great performance, hold their direct reports to account or advise them to improve performance deficits that they see during monitoring, receive their direct reports' best advice on issues, and ensure that they have communicated their positions clearly.

8. Effective Assessment

Formal reviews of performance that let employees know how effective they have been working on the tasks delegated by their managers and where they stand with the manager and the corporation.

9. Selection and Integration

Increasing the capability of the team: getting a new person into a role through a process by which a manager defines the work of a role, determines the characteristics of a person who might be successful in it and screens candidates for hiring. The hiring decision is the manager's, with the MoR's approval.

10. Deselection and Dismissal

Removing a direct report from a role for not working effectively in it, subject to a review process. Deselection is initiated by the manager. This is different from dismissal, where the employee is fired from the company for serious breach of policy. A manager deselects an employee and sends him or her as an available resource to his own manager (the deselected employee's manager-once-removed). The MoR can find another position in the organization or tell the manager to begin dismissal proceedings, following company policy. Note that the manager delivers the news of dismissal or deselection to his or her direct report. This is not done by proxies such as HR.

11. Continuous Improvement

The examination of the methods used to get work done with the purpose of finding ways to do the work at a higher level of quality, greater speed and/or lower cost. It is the purview of the manager to be continually focused on this; the manager needs to put improvement into every task and job they assign.

The Management Super-Levers

Let's explore six of the eleven general management practices – the ones I call management super-levers: context setting; task assignment; monitoring; coaching; selection and integration; and deselection and dismissal.

Context Setting of Intent, Situation and Plan

How many times a year do your managers take the opportunity to set context for their employees? Every time they do, they are using a super-lever for aligning them with the company's – with the CEO's – strategy.

If your managers do so consistently throughout the year and throughout your organization, your employees will know all they need to know to do their work. They will know what the strategy is, how their work fits and contributes to achieving it and the challenges that stand in the way of their department's or division's success. Context setting connects them to the company by telling them three key pieces of information:

- The *situation*: current circumstances in all areas relevant to the work, often both inside and outside the organization
- Your *intent* as their manager: what your direct reports' manager-once-removed wants to accomplish
- Your overall *plan* for them in their roles

Managers should set different contexts for the work of their team: as a whole, for each role and for the tasks they assign. They should also set context in every single meeting they attend. When they are not able to be present at a meeting, they should make the overall context clear to their direct reports beforehand.

If you want all of your employees to understand how they fit in and contribute to implementing your strategy, ensure a high level and high frequency of context setting. There is absolutely no excuse for employees not to understand the context and reason for their work.

Do you consistently and persistently hold all of your managers to account to do this? How dare you not! At some levels, management is just common sense, and this is one example. Managers must communicate with their employees consistently and clearly. Communication is a manager's accountability.

Do you consistently role-model this and ensure that it happens? How dare you not! This is not work for a communications department; it is a manager's work. To manage hundreds of employees effectively, you must ensure that your managers set context for them.

The ultimate accountability for context setting – and the judgment of how much is sufficient – belongs to the employee's immediate manager. Tri-level teams can be a significant aid in context setting, because the employees' "manager's manager" helps to ensure alignment and understanding. There is no information that employees need for success that cannot come from their manager. If you see employees who are confused about your strategy and out of alignment with it, look no farther than their manager. Work back up the organization, and you will discover the level of management that has failed to set clear context.

Context setting gives your employees the clarity they require and the ability to work towards the strategy even when things change on the ground. The results are immediate and powerful. Yet some managers seem oblivious to the art of context setting; they avoid this practice, usually because they are not capable in their roles.

Think about the impact on your organization were all your managers to set a clear context for your employees. What difference would it make to the alignment and implementation of the organization's strategic work?

Task Assignment

The second management super-lever is the practice of task assignment. Task assignment is not simply passing out simple lists of things to do. It is the manager's communication to a direct report that he or she is accountable to work effectively in producing a particular output and provides clearly stated QQTRs for the task.

Earlier in chapter 9, when we looked at defining work, I reviewed the importance of clear QQTRs. If context and purpose, on the one hand, and dialogue, on the other, are the pieces of bread, QQTRs are the meat in the task assignment sandwich:

1. Quantity: How much output is expected?

2. Quality: What are the objectives and subjective standards a manager deems important?

3. Time: By when must the task be completed?

4. Resources: What resources does the direct report require to assist them in the completion of the task?

To reiterate, every task a manager assigns must have QQTRs attached to make perfectly clear what is required *before* the task is delivered. When you implement them throughout an organization, QQTRs change the tenor of the conversation between employees and managers. This process makes managers clarify the priority of the work and the resources available. Employees are expected to give their best advice in response and signal their acceptance and understanding of the work being delegated to them. This process exposes any potential misunderstandings that could derail successful completion of the work. It enables a truthful dialogue between manager and direct report about work and performance.

Think of how many tasks are delegated in your company each month. What would the effect be in terms of results if this management act were consistently and professionally performed? Multiply clear understanding of accountability and authority across hundreds of employees, hold them to account and you will enable your organization to achieve its strategy.

Monitoring and Coaching

The next two super-levers among the general management practices are monitoring and coaching.

Managers can monitor their employees' work in a meaningful way once they have set the context and assigned clear QQTRs. Otherwise, there is nothing formally linked to strategy implementation to monitor or coach, and performance cannot be reviewed. Without these fundamental management disciplines in place, the focus and execution of your strategy will dissipate and falter.

Monitoring output means keeping track of what employees produce. Managers need to assess how effectively their direct reports are working in the tasks they have assigned them. If managers do not monitor, they are not managing.

Some employees automatically complain of being micromanaged when their manager monitors their work. They miss the point. They are doing work delegated to them by their manager. Their manager manages them precisely by checking their progress. If managers are adding value to their employees' work, fewer employees will see monitoring as an intrusion. It's simple, really: managers organize work and have to ensure that it is completed effectively.

Coaching enables managers to use the information they've discerned from monitoring to reinforce success as well as help employees improve any performance deficits. Coaching works through dialogue with the employee about their work: the manager advises the employee on ways to improve, and the employee offers best advice on the work through his or her perspective in doing the work. Coaching ensures that direct reports know what their manager thinks of their performance and how it can be improved.

Monitoring and coaching cannot be effective without clear role definitions, accountabilities, authorities and specified QQTRs. These are the managers' reference points. Levelling the organization simplifies the monitoring and coaching processes, because managers have only direct reports who are cognitively capable, are the right fit-to-role and can keep up with and understand their manager. Good performance and poor performance become easier to define.

Practice makes it instinctual. Think about when you learned to drive and how laborious it was. Practice has boosted your skill and confidence so that now much of your driving is directed by your subconscious: you draw on your experience, which enables you to anticipate situations and drive though hazardous situations with confidence. You need to get to the same place with these practices. These practices are part of the craft of management. They are timeless. They are the practices you use year-in and year-out to manage your business. You hold your managers clearly accountable to use them effectively.

Doing so will give your employees clarity about what is expected from them and a consistent experience of how they are managed. Remember that your employees at the lower levels of your organization crave clarity and consistency. Give it to them!

Ensure that your managers can add value to their direct reports' work. Do you remember working for a manager you did not respect? All of us have had this experience. The reason for your disrespect was either a significant difference in values or the awareness that you were brighter than they are – they were incapable of adding value to your work. They were in fact a waste of your time to talk to. So you disengaged.

You are accountable to ensure that all of the managers in your organization can add value to their employees' work. In doing this you have actually differentiated the manager from the employees they manage. You have created space between the two levels that can be filled in with value.

Think of the opposite case, in which a manager clearly cannot add value to their employees' work. They feel harried, closed in, threatened, foolish, defensive. They find their ideas and direction insufficient to be able to build respect and willingness to follow. They regard best advice as a threat because it is given to them by an employee who can out-think them and in doing so intimidates them. They often feel rejected, and are quietly or not-so-quietly ridiculed.

It is almost impossible to work effectively under these circumstances. For the management practices to be effective, employees have to feel that their manager is adding value to their work.

Managerial accountability versus employee effectiveness. Employees are assessed not on their outputs but on whether they did the work effectively. It is the manager who is accountable for poor output from his or her team. Managers cannot blame their employees for failing to deliver the results. The manager's conversation with them must be about their effectiveness. Managers coach their less effective employees to build their capability to work more effectively. If all avenues have been covered to improve performance, the manager must remove the employee from the role.

Some managers may continue to fail to meet output expectations; if so, their ability to do managerial work must be assessed. Can they build teams of engaged employees who increase in capability each year and add value to their work, enabling these managers to deliver the results from the work delegated to them? This is a manager's accountability. Think of the positive collective and cumulative impact on your organization if you get this work right.

Selection and Integration, and Deselection and Dismissal

The managerial practices of selection and deselection are super-levers available to your managers to increase the capability of their team.

Selection by managers of new team members who add value to their direct reports' work is a continuous improvement process. These managers see a gap in performance and work to fill it, unlike a struggling manager who cannot add value and who cannot see the gap. Through the selection practice, managers boost the capability of their teams with new talent.

Thorough due diligence to solve the concern must occur prior to deselection and include truthful coaching and corrective discussions. The MoR may then decide to place the deselected employee into another role or begin the process of dismissal. Like pruning a grapevine, this process is trying but necessary to create vigour and growth. Some direct reports just don't fit. They must be pruned from the organization so they can find a position where they can excel, and be replaced by an individual of higher capability.

As CEO, your accountability is to ensure that all managers in your organization can add value to the work of their direct reports and continually increase the capability of their teams – just as you should be doing, too.

Accountability and Consequences

Removing an employee is tough work for managers to do because it brings up issues of accountability and consequences. Consequences are the manager's ultimate tool to ensure that work gets done, and they can be positive or negative.

Once the QQTRs and behavioural expectations have been set, the manager must hold truthful conversations about lack of effectiveness or subpar performance with direct reports. A manager is required to be present, calm, focused and truthful. Very direct, instructive and constructive discussions can happen about performance when you encapsulate this process with respect, care and dignity. When dismissal occurs, the ante gets raised and feelings of courage, consideration and sadness will help or hinder this discussion.

Dismissing Isn't Easy, but It's Your Job

No one but a sociopath likes to fire people.

Jos Wintermans knows the pain most managers feel when they come to this task. In 1995, he spoke with the CBC about his early days at CTAL when he had to let sixteen of the top managers go.

"It's a very agonizing and traumatic experience. It's not an easy thing to do personally … It really took a toll. I felt very, very bad about it. But at the same time, it was balanced by the notion that I really felt I was putting together an organization to survive and 500 jobs were not going to be in jeopardy because of that change.

"On the one side, yes, I had pain. But on the other side I also had this purpose, which I thought was a better kind of overall approach to get the business to move."

As CEO, you are accountable for making sure employees have managers who add value. Don't let people who cannot do the work stay in the role. It's unfair to everyone in the organization under them and, ultimately, to the manager, too, because you are denying that person work where he or she can be successful.

As CEO, you should demand truthful discussions about consequences. You start with your tri-level team, where you can see and experience first-hand the quality and truth of the dialogue. You need to build your top tri-level team to role-model this behaviour in the organization. And above all you must role-model it yourself. Only then will truthful, beneficial discussions about performance start to emanate and spread through the organization.

The Foundations of the General Management Practices

It is not enough to know the eleven practices. They must become integral to how you and your managers manage. This happens through mastering the two foundations of these practices, *dialogue* and *judgment and discretion*. If you think of managers as players in a jazz group, the two foundations would not be considered their technique – their skill on their instruments – but their ear: their ability to listen to what the others are playing, to interpret the melody when it's their time to play a solo, to sit it out when someone else is hot.

Management with a KISS

KISS it (Keep It Short and Simple). Time and again I encounter over-complicated leadership models backed up with competency processes. Despite good intentions, over-busy managers don't really have the time to get their heads around the model. As a result, few managers in the organization, including the executive team, can explain or even recall the model. Managers default to their past experience and preferences in how to manage. This unleashes on employees a set of inconsistent management processes and practices and varying levels of expertise. It undermines and unsettles them and fails to consistently reinforce any management structure and practices that employees can identify with.

Our experience is that it's best if you KISS management models and make them simple and focused on a few key practices. This enables you to demand expertise and consistency from your managers as they practice the "few" management practices. Expertise is developed from doing something a thousand times!

Edward S. Kennedy, CEO of The North West Company, understands this. Managing 7,000 employees in the global business is not easy. North West chose a set of simple yet powerful management practices and uses them consistently throughout the organization. The focus on the "fewer practices" enables managers, spread over huge geographic distances, to get their heads around them and practice them in depth – developing individual and global management expertise. For North West, consistency in managerial practices is critical for both managers and employees, and is a key foundation for its expansion plans.

Dialogue

You implement the general management practices in dialogue with your employees. Strategy creation requires the best advice of your direct reports. You must dialogue with your team to define the functional structure for your strategy. Defining the work becomes an ongoing dialogue of clarification between managers and their direct reports. Lateral authorities get worked out by the management team as they enter dialogue together. The tri-level meetings, key to aligning your organization, give space for a strategic implementation of dialogue between three levels of management.

Dialogue Versus Discussion

Dialogue is a frank, respectful exploration of the assumptions being used to solve an issue. It is about learning, not being right. In dialogue, you seek to understand. A typical question in dialogue is, "On what do you base this opinion or insight?" The rule is that I can challenge you for clarity and understanding, as in, "How did you reach this conclusion?" Dialogue is very useful when dealing with a complex issue. It helps sort it out. Dialogue solicits best advice and enlists employees in understanding issues and generating solutions. Participants in dialogue learn.

Discussion is used to come to a decision. Discussion rhymes with percussion. It's a persuasive conversation by which you try to close things down, prove a point, test hard and make a decision. Discussion is essential to successful management, but it needs to be used adeptly. Discussion used early in problem solving can shut the conversation down too fast, heading off the possibility of a more effective, even groundbreaking solution.

As CEO, you need to balance the use of dialogue and discussion.

Through dialogue, you pursue the truth of an issue, and this requires courage. An assumption behind an important decision may be exposed as wrong. All thinking is examined to understand the assumptions it is based on and to expose any flaws in the previous thinking.

Dialogue with your team can be challenging when there are multiple levels of capability. Team members can misunderstand one another or become overwhelmed and left behind in the dialogue. Levelling the organization makes dialogue easier and more effective because it ensures a similar level of thinking among team members. Team members understand one another, can keep up with one another and are comfortable exploring issues, challenges and concepts of the same level of complexity.

Judgment and Discretion

All of the work of the first six CEO management principles can be severely compromised, even destroyed, unless managers manage and make it happen.

Managerial work is the exercise of judgment and discretion while engaged in a task; there are aspects of the work world that are tangible and can be measured easily, and other aspects that can only be judged. The subjective judgment part of management can be uncomfortable. Your managers will be called on to judge how effectively their direct reports work; this is something they do subjectively all the time.

- Judgment: The choosing of one path over another
- Discretion: The authority to exercise judgment

The general management practices simply bring judgment and discretion out into the open. For example, as mentioned in the previous chapter, if you ask any of your direct reports to rank their direct reports in order of capability, they will know the answer, and it will be correct. However, managers are not well practiced in justifying their subjective views. In fact, consulting firms have created a whole series of objective processes that enable managers to avoid the discomfort of justifying a subjective judgment. Ask managers if they feel certain that their direct reports are being paid fairly. They will have an opinion. Ask them to justify to lower-paid employees why their pay is less than that of their colleagues, and they will be more comfortable using *measurement*, e.g., the Hay compensation system (saying, "It's the system that dictates what you are paid"), than *judgment* (saying, "For the performance I receive from you, this is what I think you are worth").

Dialogue and judgment and discretion go together like nuts and bolts in effective work at all levels of an organization. As Wilfred Brown, the long-serving CEO of Glacier Metal and British Minister of Trade, said forty years ago, "Work done by human beings normally calls for the use of some judgement."[29]

To get work done, all employees require discretion: the ability to use their faculties of judgment, informed by expertise and learning. Working with others in an organization requires regular dialogue.

Most of the time, dialogue and judgment are useless without each other. Studies have borne this out. For example, Kathleen Eisenhardt of Stanford University studied executive teams in the always-changing computing industry who could make fast strategic decisions versus those who made slow ones. Her findings showed that, in each fast-moving company, the CEO included his or her executive team in the decision-making process. As far as these CEOs were concerned, if consensus could be reached – great. If not, they made the tough calls about strategic direction.[30]

You need to have both together, dialogue and judgment. You join others in dialogue, especially at executive levels, to get their best advice and try to achieve consensus. But at some point, you may need to move the dialogue to discussion and make the decision. That's your call as the manager.

Action Steps

1. Examine the state of the management skills of your management team.

   a. Do you have a set of management practices that are used uniformly by all of your managers?

    b. Can you quote all of these practices by heart? (If not, what's the point of them?)

    c. How well do you practice them yourself? Are you and your team great role models?

2. What steps will you take to maximize the impact of your management team to enable all of your employees to contribute to achieving your strategy?

3. What management practices would you use as super-levers in your organization?

Executive Summary

1. Management makes everything happen in your organization. You can follow the first six CEO management principles, but without the seventh – effective management – everything will fall apart.

2. Keep the general management practices simple and focused on a few, because:
- Managers can get their heads around a few
- It makes it easier for employees to feel they are being managed consistently
- The repeated practice of a few builds expertise and skill

3. Hold employees accountable. Ensure that truthful conversations with consequences occur.

4. Imagine the effect on your employees if all of your managers effectively and consistently set context throughout your organization.

PART THREE

Keeping the Gap Closed

CHAPTER ELEVEN

Protecting the Sacred Manager–Direct Report Relationship

To this point we have explored the CEO skill gap and how to close it. As we come to the end of this book, the question of sustainability looms large. That question is how you, as CEO, can keep your skill gap closed, and in doing so, help close the skill gaps of your entire organization.

This work starts and ends with you. It never ends. It is CEO work. It is your "just another day at the office." As CEO, you are the ultimate manager of managers from whom all accountability flows, for you create the strategy with your executives and then hold them accountable to deliver major parts of this strategy through the function they head. They, in turn, do the same with their direct reports.

The Sacred Relationship of Your Organization

Sustainability flows directly from your protection and nurture of the manager–direct report relationship, the sacred relationship of an organization. Organizations thrive, plane or even die depending on the health of this relationship. The chief reason employees leave a company is a dysfunctional relationship with their immediate manager. Your job is to ensure that this relationship is highly functional.

Accountability versus Responsibility

Earlier in this book I made a distinction between accountability and responsibility. (See page 51.) I defined the former as "a contract between managers and their direct reports" and the latter as "a feeling of obligation and caring, which, if it is not tied to account-ability, can end at the level of feeling ... and may or may not lead to action." Consider how many manager–direct report relation-ships there are in your organization. It will be a large number, in the hundreds or thousands. Each one is a costly investment by you. It is critically important for you to clarify the language that's used in this relationship. Companies succeed when every employee is working on what their managers hold them accountable to do – not on what they choose to do.

RESPONSIBILITY   ACCOUNTABILITY

Responsibility is a   Accountability is a
personal feeling of obligation component of a relationship

"What I FEEL I should do"   "What my manager
                               wants me to do"

Figure 44: Responsibility versus accountability.

Avoid Cormorant Management

One way you can protect the sacred manager–direct report relation-ship is to model for managers of managers a refusal to dive down and change, alter or otherwise interfere with the work of their managers' direct reports. I call this cormorant management™, a practice that is unfair to managers because it prevents them from being held accountable for results. Quite rightly, their feeling is, "How can you hold me accountable for the outputs of my employees when you dive down and change the priority of my direct reports' work?"

The idea of accountability is to delegate work by defining the end state you require and then allowing employees the space and authority to get it done without interference. This enables employees to think for themselves and learn how to deliver work to their manager. What managers of managers lose on the roundabout by working through the system instead of by divine fiat, they will gain on the straightaway as competence and trust drive results throughout the organization.

Some time ago I was working with an organization and introduced them to the process of accountability. I talked about the accountabilities of managers versus those of their boss and told them their boss's boss cannot give them tasks directly; delegation should come through their immediate managers. There was a great stirring in the group. One of the employees left the room without explanation. On his return, he shared with the group a picture that he had just created. He had printed a photo of the EVP in charge (a full four levels above the employee in question). He had superimposed a red circle on the photo with a line through it; the caption read, "You are NOT the boss of me!" It was a gutsy response. Everyone in the room understood immediately.

It turned out that this EVP regularly bypassed the management in this employee's department and went straight to the analysts, demanding updated information. This interference upset the department's timely delivery of work. It also undermined the team's manager because the request from this executive was seen to be more important work than what the manager had assigned them. The EVP in question saw the sign (it was soon posted everywhere in his division) and changed his behaviour and started working through his direct reports.

Use Dialogue and Best Advice – All the Time!

As discussed earlier (see pages 172–75), managers strengthen and enhance their relationship with their direct reports by dialoguing with their reports and encouraging them to give their best advice. Make sure, when dialogue is used throughout your organization, that your strategy is explained, impractical strategic assumptions are culled out and employees become a central part of the implementation of strategy. When best advice is given throughout your organization, upward communication is encouraged (versus the traditional top-down communication found in many companies).

Managers cannot be expected to have all of the answers; they require assistance. In the Mike Myers movie *Austin Powers: International Man of Mystery*, Dr. Evil has just been thawed out after twenty years of cryogenic freezing. Meeting with his henchman to discuss the next big global heist, he proposes a series of outdated ideas (create a hole in the ozone layer, suggest that Prince Charles has had an affair ...). Each time, his Number Two tells him that it has already happened. In frustration, Dr. Evil exclaims, "Throw me a frickin' bone!" He personifies the aggravation managers feel in the face of trying to solve an issue and not getting sufficient best advice.

Best advice lies at the heart of the creation and sustainment of an effective organization. It is a key contributor to building that critical manager–direct report relationship. It is the "other" dimension in the relationship. Managers have the accountability to delegate; direct reports have the accountability to comment and engage in fashioning the best solution. Best advice is the key to creating a proactive organization rather than a passive one. Your employees' opinions matter. Your managers have to be big enough in their roles to have the confidence to engage openly with their direct reports and hear what they have to say and explain why they agree or disagree. When managers receive best advice, they don't have to agree with it. But for the sake of building a respectful, productive relationship with their direct reports, they should explain why.

How Are You Doing? An Exercise

To sustain success, make it a habit to constantly monitor how effective your relationships are with each of your direct reports. Are you clearly specifying the tasks you have delegated, using QQTRs (or a similar method) to specify the work they're accountable for? Are you engaging them in healthy dialogue? Are you receiving sufficient best advice so you can verify that the context and outputs for the delegated task are clearly understood?

1. Calculate how many individual manager–direct report relationships you have in your organization.

How healthy are they?

---

2. Do you have a clear and fair process for holding your employees accountable? Describe it.

---

3. Do you get your employees to give their full best advice? Do you get fair value from them for the salaries you pay them?

Executive Summary

1. The key relationship – the sacred relationship – in your organization is the manager–direct report relationship. Your

organization, and your organization's success, depends on how healthy this relationship is.

2. Understand the difference between "accountability" and "responsibility." They mean two very different things. Remember, clear language is important in effective management. Accountability is a contract between you and a direct report to complete a task. Responsibility is a feeling of obligation and caring. It can undermine the implementation of your strategy.

3. If you hold your managers accountable to deliver results, be sure you are not a cormorant manager. Remember, only your managers can give their direct reports work. This authority enables them to build trusting relationships.

4. All management should be practiced in dialogue.

5. Ensure that best advice thrives throughout your organization. Hold all employees accountable to give it. Get your money's worth of best advice.

CHAPTER TWELVE

Transcending the Number-One Block to CEO Success

We have just discussed how sustainability of success in an organization depends on the health of the sacred manager–direct report relationship. The second key to sustainability is having truthful conversations. I end the book on this note because failing to have these conversations is the number-one block to CEO success.

Early on in my career, I was given the project to design and implement a program across the company on behalf of the CEO that would engage 6,000 employees in dialogue to explain and clarify the CEO's strategy.

I had a key direct report who was crucial in helping design the materials and process to successfully implement the project. But the problem was that she had a fearful, negative attitude – an emotional inconsistency that was very hard to manage. I chose accommodation and conciliation and avoided truthful conversations about goals and consequences. As a result of my approach, she nearly killed the project and my career.

It was entirely my fault, because I chose not to confront her, clarify my expectations and hold her accountable for her lack of effectiveness and behaviour. I never forgot that lesson: the requirement to be direct and clear and hold employees to the required standards of productivity and behaviour.

In their book *Preparing CEOs for Success*, Leslie W. Braksick and James S. Hillgren asked CEOs what they wished they had known before taking on the assignment. A telling quote follows; the thought it expresses should be a cornerstone for everything you do in your role: "I think a big challenge of the CEO role is addressing people issues promptly and decisively. If you are not going to face and deal with the people issues, you have no business saying 'yes' to the job of CEO."[31]

You must be capable of having these truthful conversations so you can act as a role model for your entire organization. As CEO, you are accountable to ensure a work environment in which employees can apply their full capability to their work, including critical thinking, and an environment in which they can challenge those "sacred cows" that are preventing the company from achieving competitive advantage and growth.

I am always amazed at the number of people at the top of organizations who cannot or will not have truthful conversations about performance. When it comes to task and work issues, they can be quite animated, but on people and performance issues they are silent. They hold back and avoid uncomfortable conversations about the truth.

Nobody wants to hear bad news or be the messenger bearing it, but the inability of CEOs to tell the truth about poor performance is bad news for the organization they lead. These CEOs create a huge roadblock to the potential success of their organization.

The thought of having truthful conversations about performance with your direct reports may make you very uncomfortable. You may be resistant to the idea of accepting their best advice, especially when they point out that something you want done won't work with the QQTR you demand (Quantity, Quality, Time, Resources). Bottom line: avoidance of truthful conversations is probably the most significant cause of CEO failure.

Anaklesis: The Number-One Management Disease

There is a single problem that underlies all of these excuses. Each one can be traced back to a single root, one that compromises dialogue, discretion and clarity. It is the single most common disease in management today.

I call it *anaklesis*, from the Greek meaning "to lean on." My colleague Herb Koplowitz and author Jerry Harvey define the term as leaning on concepts and relationships to make sense of the world as a place where we can get our needs met. I extend the term to describe, in the context of management, the dangerous dependency on concepts and relationships that can lead to organizational dysfunction.

Anaklesis describes managers' decision not to confront under-performance or hold hard, truthful conversations with direct reports because they fear they will threaten work relationships. It describes clinging to weak systems, definitions or processes – even when we know they are wrong – in order to avoid cognitive dissonance.

Behaviours Anaklitic Management Will Avoid
• Judging someone's work as unacceptable
• Telling employees they do not have the potential to be promoted
• Bringing news to the board about a late project
• Demanding that a key employee must do more with less
• Pointing out the "stinking, rotten moose head" in a meeting when everyone is ignoring it
• Aligning and integrating the work of silos with executives who don't want to be team players
• Ensuring that key policies are followed by all of the executive team to ensure clear, consistent management for all employees
• Calling out mediocre performance in the organization; removing under-performing executives from their roles; holding discussions about poor performance
• Ensuring that points are discussed, argued and tested vociferously at the executive table to get the best solution
• Confronting senior executives who are fighting and playing political games

What Anaklesis Can Do to an Organization

How many of the above examples apply to your company? How many apply to one or more of your direct reports? And how many apply to your handling of performance issues at work?

As the CEO goes, so goes the company.

The hesitation to speak the truth, the desire to shade the truth and put it in a more acceptable light and the avoidance of the truth combine to lock the organization into carefully sanitized discussions that breed mediocre performance, lost opportunity and disengaged employees. To allow this as a CEO is to compromise yourself in your management role.

You can see how this creates damage. Senior executives in the organization are unaligned and unmanaged. The process of aligning and integrating the strategic work of the organization breaks down. Bickering between senior executives exacerbates anaklitic behaviour in the two reporting levels below them, as direct reports try to navigate through complex issues while still being seen to be supporting the unreasonable behaviour of their boss. Initiatives begin to bog down. Conversation becomes political and adversarial as employees mirror the behaviour of their managers.

This is all because the CEO is anaklitic and will not call out these behaviours or deliver the required consequences. Anaklesis is like a thick fog that settles over the organization, quietly choking off its air.

In one senior leadership team with which I worked, Claude (not his real name), an executive vice president, complained about one of his direct reports. The rest of the executive team agreed that this employee was ineffective and not capable of doing the thinking the role required. They said he needed to be removed from the role.

Claude just shrugged. "I know you're right," he said. "I gave him a piece of work that had to go to the CEO. It was so bad when I got it back that I spent two days redoing it."

What a waste of time, doing your direct report's work for them! Claude was distracted from doing the work of an executive for two days as a result. Claude was anaklitic: his excessive reliance on his relationship with this employee left him incapable of having a truthful conversation about performance. Fortunately for the rest of his team – and for that non-performing manager's own direct reports – this inability led to Claude's replacement soon afterwards. His manager was not anaklitic.

In extreme situations, executives have used the anaklitic dependencies of others to do as they will in the organization. They skilfully play on their superiors' reluctance to be truthful and continue down their path of destruction.

How dare you let these things happen! As CEO, you must be a manager who values and expects truthful conversations in everything you do. You must demonstrate that you value people by the way they engage with courage, character and humility as they listen, explain and solicit the truth from those with whom they work.

Too many CEOs need to stiffen their backbone and show more character. They need to stop hiding behind the status of their office and the sycophantic realm they have created around them where the truth dies in service to an emperor who wears no clothes.

Anaklesis and HR

It may seem that I've been unfair to HR in this book, making sure that it doesn't encroach on what is properly the CEO's purview. (See pages 31, 71, 156, 164.) Here, however, I wish to point out how anaklesis actually compromises HR and promotes a misunderstanding of HR's role.

Many HR functions are staffed by caring individuals who think they are helping when they are actually undermining that critical manager–direct report relationship and therefore management's ability to get work done. Managers often do not understand the craft of management and their accountabilities as a manager. Managers dump their uncomfortable work on these well-intentioned HR employees, who are enthusiastic about helping. In doing this, managers enlist HR in a complicit circle of dependency that enables managers to avoid the required anaklitic discussions of performance with their employees. HR unwittingly undermines that key relationship of the organization.

This is not HR's function. HR is an administrative and support role for you and your managers. It does no management work other than in its own function. In the scenario above, it has been forced into filling a void caused by managers' abdication of their managerial work. Holding truthful conversations about performance is the accountability of managers, not HR.

You cannot allow your managers – or yourself – to lob these issues over the wall to HR. HR employees become the enablers of your managers. By usurping the role of the immediate manager, they drive a wedge between managers and their direct reports, debilitating the key trust-building relationship in your organization. If you let your managers lean on HR to avoid the uncomfortable work of management, you give anaklesis room to grow and undermine managers' energy and strength to get things done.

This anaklitic dependency on HR is driven by the heavy weight of wrongheaded assumptions and practices elsewhere in the organization. Managers must manage. It is managers who must define the work of their direct reports and the authorities and accountabilities it requires as well as ensure their welfare. This includes you as the top manager of your organization.

You are accountable for hiring and firing, and for building your organization's capability to get work done. You are accountable for personally having the truthful and uncomfortable conversations with your direct reports about tardiness, poor behaviour and poor performance and any consequences that may result.

All this compromises the effectiveness and agility of your organization and distracts HR from its important role of supporting the manager: providing strategic advice to the president, administering compensation and benefits, creating the systems and processes that enable your managers to manage. HR has an advisory authority with managers but should never cross the line to become a surrogate manager. Likewise, managers should never be allowed to abdicate their management accountabilities and authorities by leaning on HR.

The Other Side of Anaklesis

Anaklesis not only keeps us from confronting poor performance in our direct reports, it also keeps everyone below the CEO from giving the manager best advice. As discussed earlier (pages 172–75 and 181–82), employees are accountable to help their managers make better decisions by giving them their best advice on work issues.

All employees come to work to contribute, but often the organization sends mixed messages about wanting to hear their opinions. Do you truly want to hear best advice from your employees? In my experience, executives who dare to manage want best advice but cannot seem to get it. Are you getting good value in best advice for what you are paying? Are you creating a environment that supports best advice being given to you?

What is your level of anaklesis? What is the level of anaklesis in your executive/senior management team? Anaklesis is often the reason for lack of candid discussion on the top team. How fruitful are your conversations with direct reports? Are they often tinged with caution and compromise because you don't want to offend or marginalize?

I have to say that in my years of working at the executive level in companies, anaklesis *flourishes* at the executive table. Those who reach the executive rank often exhibit behaviours driven by insecurity, fear of losing stock options/bonuses, fear of failure, a need to win or dominate, a flagrant disregard for others and sometimes even sociopathic tendencies – any or all of which will undermine the ability of a senior team to work together effectively. Anaklesis grows like algae in a pond, eventually suffocating any life in the water.

The most common response I get when I discuss anaklesis with CEOs is silence. Over the years I have come to understand that this silence means something like: "I have managed to avoid the really awkward conversations up till now. I'm not sure how to do it, and the thought of doing it makes me feel very uncomfortable." I learn that leaders of industry lie awake at night fretting over having uncomfortable conversations. They are actually human! The following exercise illustrates the structure I give them for such conversations, to remind them that these conversations are fundamental to their work.

Your Company and Truthful Conversations: An Exercise

What is the state of truthful conversations in your organization? Score it on the following scale:

1. Totally truthful – nothing is held back.

2. Open – will share the uncomfortable truths, but worried how to do it, so the process sometimes falters and we do not share all.

3. Will share somewhat, but caution prevails.

4. Guarded – will say little. What is said is couched in very careful terms.

5. Closed – avoids everything.

Any score between 3 and 5 should be considered unacceptable.

If your assessment is between 3 and 5, and given what you have read in the last two chapters, what can you do to correct this?

_____

_____

_____

If your assessment is between 1 and 2, what can you do to reinforce it?

_____

_____

Executive Summary

1. An organization in which managers and employees do not have truthful conversations loses efficiency, effectiveness and trust between everyone who works there.

2. Anaklesis is a common management dysfunction. It sucks the oxygen out of the culture. Your managers need to display courage to overcome it.

3. Be clear about HR's role: HR does not manage the company. It must not compromise the manager–direct report relationship.

4. Support HR. Do not let your managers lob uncomfortable truthful conversations over the wall to them. It is your managers' work. Hold them to account to behave as managers.

Conclusion

So what do the results of a company that has adopted the seven CEO management principles look like over the long term? Just consider what happened at CTAL/CTFS from 1992 to 2011, where four successive CEOs saw the value of the philosophy of the structure they inherited and stayed the course. The results:

- Growth in net credit charge receivables: $3.4 billion, or almost seven times the value of the company in 1992
- Achieved $953 million in Gross Operating Revenues by 2011, up from $191 million in 1992
- A significant reduction in operating expenses as a percentage of credit charge receivables
- An increase in Income Before Taxes of almost 400%
- And all of this presided over by a well-planned and well-executed succession plan

What kind of company can achieve that phenomenal success? A company that holds to an optimal number of levels structurally and is led by a CEO who sets the enterprise strategy, defines the organization's core function and how all other functions serve it, places highly capable men and women over these functions to report to the CEO, frees employees to do great work and builds and maintains a culture of accountability, relentlessly challenging and maintaining the required capability to drive to achieving that strategy. A company that excels has the capability to successfully take on complex initiatives and the agility to respond to the ever-changing economic climate and the confidence to balance growth with the financial risks in the face of stiff competition. A company that excels in succession planning produces a long list of executive leaders who will fill key roles in the executive suite.

Figure 45: The pain of change.

If you are ready to start doing this work, what's getting in your way? Figure 45 highlights the dilemma. If you focus on the seven CEO management principles with perseverance, tenacity and consistency, you can transform your company to achieve the future you desire.

But no change happens unless your desire for the outcome and the outcome itself outweigh the pain of getting there — the pain of some managers' and employees' resistance to change; the pain of an initial dip in company profits; the pain of receiving tough feedback.

You will have to change many of your own ideas. You will have to do the hard work of unlearning parts of your old version of management reality for what is espoused in the CEO management principles. This reminds me of when I first learned to snowboard. I was fine for several years with the methods I had initially learned. However, when I wanted to step up to the next level, I was told that many of my snowboarding habits were actually preventing me from progressing. I had to unlearn my old methods so I could adopt better ones. It was painful and exhausting, but it worked.

The same is true here. Yes, starting to follow the craft of management is hard work and requires many changes. But your knowledge and skills will evolve over time. (Remember KASH: knowledge, attitudes, skills and habits.)

Creating an efficient, effective and fair place to work requires speaking the truth in some uncomfortable circumstances. The dissonance of discontent can stifle change and wear you down. This is where courage counts. You want to be more than just a placeholder CEO; you want to be one of the great ones. Stop the fads, learn the craft and build a great company.

To get started, review and put into action the seven CEO management principles in order. Principles 1 to 5 set the foundations for great performance; principles 6 and 7 enable the performance to happen. In doing this work, never lose sight of the number of employees in your company and your mandate as CEO to become an expert in understanding how to positively affect their immediate world. Why hire them unless you pay particular attention to ensuring that their productivity is maximized?

The end of each chapter covering a CEO management principle (chapters 4–10) included a section of Action Step questions. Your answers should give you deeper insight into the current state of your organization and what is blocking it from achieving its full potential. Go back and review your answers.

Chapter	Title	Topic
Chapter 4	Principle #1: Create Your Strategy	Is your strategy real and clear to your employees?

Chapter 5	Principle #2: Choose Your Organization's Functional Structure	Is your core function clarified?
Chapter 6	Principle #3: Level the Organization	Do you have too many layers? Too few?
Chapter 7	Principle #4: Define the Work	Do your employees understand what work they're accountable for?
Chapter 8	Principle #5: Manage Your Organization's Lateral Relationships	Do your employees have the authority required to complete the work that is required by strategy?
Chapter 9	Principle #6: Build the Required Talent	Do you have the required employee capability at each level of your organization to successfully implement your strategy?
Chapter 10	Principle #7: Make It All Happen with Effective Management	Do you have a simple, effective, common set of management practices used uniformly across your organization?

Mastering the Craft of Management Will Enable You to:

- Become a successful CEO
- Win a reputation as a manager capable of positively transforming organizations and lives
- Build a sustainable organization – one that transcends you
- Set your company on a path of innovation and creative problem solving

- Watch your organization become sustainably profitable

The Results of This Work Will Include:

- Your strategy is achieved
- Your company is a great place to work – it is fair and trusting
- Your company is more effective at retaining, attracting and developing top talent
- Employees feel safe and valued
- Employees are contributing members who innovate and engage their customers
- The company is known for its innovation and problem-solving ability
- Work is done faster and more efficiently
- Projects come in on time, on target
- Profitability increases
- Shareholder value increases

The Benefits to Managers:

- They have the authority to use their direct reports as a resource and the skills to do that respectfully
- No one else interferes with their use of their direct reports
- There isn't anyone on their team they don't want there
- They can delegate the work that is below their level of capability
- They can diagnose an organizational problem and solve it without creating a problem elsewhere
- They consider it fair to hold them accountable

The Benefits to Employees:

- They know what they are expected to do, and it is work they find challenging yet within their capability
- They know their authorities, and they are sufficient for them to meet their accountabilities
- They are managed by someone more capable than they are

- Their pay is fair for the level of challenge in their work
- They know what their future is in the organization
- They are able to escalate when they have problems
- They are treated with respect; their personal values and beliefs are not tampered with
- They believe it is fair to hold them accountable

For all of these benefits to accrue to you and your organization, you must build the most capable management team possible to serve and manage your employees. You will not be the best friend of your managers if they are ineffective in their roles. You will remove them as a service to your 250+ employees and replace them with managers of greater capability who can manage more effectively. Your employees will thank you for this verbally – and then repay your action with greater enthusiasm and productivity.

To build credibility with employees, the "line manager" is omnipotent. If all of your managers are seen to follow and practice the craft of management, then the most sacred relationship of all – that of manager and direct report – will become effective, trusting and highly productive. It is the overarching work you do through the seven CEO management principles that will make and keep relationships strong throughout your organization.

Get the principles right, and you and your company will soar.

Acknowledgments

It has been said that everyone has a book in them. Mine has been twenty-five years in the making and is the culmination of my entrepreneurial trek. But I realize and appreciatively accept that *How Dare You Manage?* would never have reached publication without the support, cajolement, perseverance, enthusiasm and expertise of so many people.

Hanging in a shabby frame on my office wall is a Calvin Coolidge quote that I treasure:

Press on.

Nothing in the world can take the place of persistence. Talent will not; nothing is more common than unsuccessful men with talent. Genius will not; unrewarded genius is almost a proverb. Education will not; the world is full of educated derelicts.

Persistence and determination alone are omnipotent.

If I ever become disheartened about a project on which I am working, this quote keeps me going strong.

I would like to express my gratitude to Michael Anderson and Herb Koplowitz, for their erudite understanding of strategic concepts and their spirited critiques; Bob Armstrong, Ron Charles, Rob Franklin, Rick Howes, Carmine Marcello, Tom O'Neill and Mary Turner, for their corporate knowledge and commentary; my Forrest colleagues Julian Chapman, Brenda Gefucia and Tony Welsh, for their valuable contributions, especially concerning actual industry applications; Forrest Christian, for graciously and patiently extricating from me the themes for the book and providing gifted direction; Michael Clark, for his powerful creative flair and conceptual direction; Lori Harrison, for translating my inadequate scribbles into coherent diagrams; Fiore Hawryluk, for her amazing, continuous coaching, encouragement, prodding, kindness and administrative support throughout my literary journey; Marsali Federico, for her sharp eye and assiduous proofreading; Alan Kay, for his advice on publishing and promotion; Edward Kennedy, for sharing with me his own views on building the best possible work environment where employees thrive; Andy Neale, for his critical read of the manuscript and his useful addition of key points on accountability; and Jos Wintermans, without whose personal insights this book would not have been possible. Jos, as the person who introduced me to the teachings of Elliott Jaques, has accompanied me on my lifelong learning of the craft of management, and I have been privileged to share in his corporate successes.

It has been a pleasure to work with my editor and publisher, Don Bastian, who is a man of deep intellect balanced with an amazing sense of tact; and my publicist, Eva Innes, who is also a cherished friend.

And there are so many other people who deserve kudos, too numerous to list all of them here (after all, this book was literally decades in the making!). These are the guests at dinner parties who didn't push away from the table when I started talking about the craft of management; the friends who found themselves unexpectedly in the middle of an argument on corporate structure; the work colleagues who listened and gave feedback when buttonholed; the wonderful clients from whom I drew strength and insight, whom I was privileged to accompany on their difficult journeys – we learned so much together: much of it is now in this book; the fellow consultants who were generous with stories from their own experiences.

Finally, I thank my family: my wife, Sally, son David and daughter Tessa. I am blessed to have the richness of their company in my life. They give me joy and keep me young.

Endnotes

1. Braksick, Leslie W. & Hillgren, James S. (2011). *Preparing CEOs for Success: What I Wish I Knew.* H.J. Heinz Company. (Kindle Locations 1478-1480). BookMasters. Kindle Edition. (To use a portion of this book, write ‹ceostudy@cdg.com›.)

2. Hodson, Randy. Cited in Osterman, Paul (2009). "Recognizing the Value of Middle Management." *Ivey Business Journal*, vol. 73, no. 6. ‹http://www.iveybusinessjournal.com/topics/global-business/recognizing-the-value-of-middle-management›. Accessed June 13, 2011.

3. See, for example, Steve Coomber (July 2005). "Henry Mintzberg: Engaging Leadership." *New Zealand Management*, vol. 52, no. 6. ‹http://www.questia.com/read/1G1-134257536›. Accessed August 30, 2012.

4. Ian McDonald, in private communication, June 2007. See also ‹http://www.roberts.edu/Academics/AcademicDivisions/BusinessManagement/msl/Community/Journal/TheHighCostofLowMorale.htm› for more on the repercussions, outside the workplace, of low morale in the workplace.

5. "Are Boards and CEOs Accountable for the Right Level of Work." *Ivey Business Journal*, May/June 2004.

6. Graham, John R., Harvey, Campbell R. & Rajgopal, Shivaram (September 6, 2006). "Value Destruction and Financial Reporting Decisions." Available at SSRN: ‹http://ssrn.com/abstract=871215› or ‹http://dx.doi.org/10.2139/ssrn.871215›.

7. Canadian Management Centre and Ispos Reid (2012)."Build a Better Workplace: Employee Engagement Edition." ‹www.cmctraining.org›.

8. Ipsos Reid (2012).‹http://www.ipsos-na.com/news-polls/pressrelease.aspx?id=5459›.

9. BlessingWhite. ‹http://www.blessingwhite.com/capabilities.asp?pid=4›.

10. Towers Watson. ‹http://www.towerswatson.com/Insights/IC-Types/Survey-Research-Results/2012/07/2012-Towers-Watson-Global-Workforce-Study›.

11. Christensen, Clayton M. & Raynor, Michael E. (2003). *The Innovator's Solution: Creating and Sustaining Successful Growth.* Cambridge, MA: Harvard Business School Press.

12. Raynor, Michael E. (2007). *The Strategy Paradox: Why Committing to Success Leads to Failure (And What to Do About It)*. New York: Crown Business, 2007.

13. Kinston, Warren & Rowbottom, Ralph (1989). *Making General Management Work in the National Health Service: A Guide to General Management for NHS Managers*. Uxbridge, UK: SIGMA Centre/Brunel University.

14. *Business World* (May 20, 2002). "The Great Leveller." ‹http://www.tata.com/company/Media/inside.aspx?artid=uDoc7sSx6RM=›. Accessed November 12, 2012.

15. Macdonald, Ian, Burke, Catherine & Steward, Karl (2006). *Systems Leadership: Creating Positive Organisations*. Burlington, VT: Gower Publishing.

16. Dutrisac, Maurice & Clement, Stephen D. (2007), pp. 186–96. "The Inglis Story: How It Became the Number One Appliance Company in Canada." In Shepard, Ken, Gray, Jerry L., Hunt, James G. (Jerry) & McArthur, Sarah (eds.). *Organization Design, Levels of Work & Human Capability: Executive Guide*. Global Organization Design Society.

17. Dive, Brian (2004). *The Healthy Organization: A Revolutionary Approach to People & Management* (2nd ed.). London: Kogan Page.

18. Drucker, Peter (1993 [1973]), p. 234. *Management: Tasks, Responsibilities, Practices*. New York: HarperBusiness.

19. Johnson, Gerry, Scholes, Kevan & Whittington, Richard (2008), p. 3 (authors' italics). *Exploring Corporate Strategy: Text & Cases* (8th ed.). Essex, UK: Pearson Educational.

20. Raynor, Michael E. (2007). *The Strategy Paradox: Why Committing to Success Leads to Failure (And What to Do About It)*. New York: Crown Business, 2007.

21. Mintzberg, Henry (1987). "The Strategy Concept I: The Five Ps for Strategy." *California Management Review*, vol. 30, no. 1.

22. Christian, E. Forrest (2008). "Become the Enablement Vehicle." Requisite Reading. The Manasclerk Company, November 3, 2008. Web November 5. ‹http://www.manasclerk.com/blog/2008/11/03/becoming-the-enablement-vehicle/›.

23. Chandler, Alfred D., Jr. (1998 [1962]). *Strategy and Structure: Chapters in the History of the American Industrial Enterprise*. Cambridge, MA: MIT Press.

24. See ‹www.prisonexp.org/psychology›.

25. Brown, Wilfred (1960), pp. 18–19. *Explorations in Management*. London: Heinemann Educational Books.

26. Osterman, Paul (2009). "Recognizing the Value of Middle Management." *Ivey Business Journal*, vol. 73, no. 6, p. 7. ‹http://www. iveybusinessjournal.com/topics/global-business/recognizing-the-value-of-middle-management›. Accessed June 13, 2011.

27. Collins, Jim (2001). *Good to Great: Why Some Companies Make the Leap … and Others Don't*. New York: HarperCollins.

28. Gaille, Brandon. (May 28, 2013). "Top Reasons Employees Leave their Jobs." ‹http://brandongaille.com/ top-reasons-employees-leave-their-jobs/›.

29. Brown, Wilfred (1971), p. 13. *Organization*. Burlington, VT: Ashgate Publishing.

30. Eisenhardt, Kathleen (1989). "Are Boards and CEOs Accountable for the Right Level of Work." *Academy of Management Journal*, vol. 32, no. 3, pp. 543–76.

31. Braksick, Leslie W. & Hillgren, James S. (2011). *Preparing CEOs for Success: What I Wish I Knew*. H.J. Heinz Company. (Kindle Locations 1478–1480). BookMasters. Kindle Edition. (To use a portion of this book, write ‹ceostudy@cdg.com›.)

Index

About Nick Forrest

Before founding Forrest & Company Limited in 1987, **Nick Forrest** spent twenty-five years in progressively senior line-management and staff roles in food manufacturing and retailing organizations in the UK and in Canada. His initial front-line management experience laid the foundation for his lifelong fascination with how great management can engage and energize large groups of employees to achieve high levels of productivity and outstanding results.

Nick has coached numerous CEOs and executives to help them achieve their management goals. This experience has given him great insight into what works and what does not work when managing large numbers of employees – insights that form the basis of his book *How Dare You Manage? Seven Principles to Close the CEO Skill Gap.*

In his book, and in his coaching and speaking, Nick addresses the significant gap in the capability of many senior executives who reach the very top, because they:

- Have never been taught how to manage large groups of employees
- Have never been accountable for everything
- Believe their role is to lead, rather than to manage

Nick is an engaging and entertaining speaker who challenges his audiences to re-examine their managerial leadership beliefs. He is an advocate for the craft of management.

Nick may be contacted by writing to nforrest@forrestandco.com.

About Forrest & Company Limited

In business since 1987, **Forrest & Company** specializes in executive management coaching and organizational transformation.

We are experts in identifying, releasing and developing leadership and organizational potential, thereby amplifying our clients' productivity and providing them with a strategic competitive advantage.

We do this by offering clients – through consulting, training, coaching and facilitation – the most effective integrated system available for organizational, team and individual transformation. We:

- Develop strategy and plan implementation
- Optimize organizations' capability to successfully implement their strategy
- Develop leadership and management ability

For more information, please contact:

Forrest & Company Limited
1300 Yonge Street, Suite 502
Toronto ON M4T 1X3
Canada
(416) 925-2967
info@forrestandco.com

www.howdareyoumanage.com
www.forrestandco.com

CPSIA information can be obtained at www.ICGtesting.com
Printed in the USA
LVOW06s1624030214

371856LV00011B/9/P